The Ultimate Personality Guide

The Ultimate Personality Guide

Jennifer Freed *and* Debra Birnbaum

Jeremy P. Tarcher/Putnam
a member of Penguin Putnam Inc.
New York

Most Tarcher/Putnam books are available at
special quantity discounts for bulk purchase for sales promotions,
premiums, fund-raising, and educational needs. Special books
or book excerpts also can be created to fit specific needs.
For details, write Putnam Special Markets,
375 Hudson Street, New York, NY 10014.

Jeremy P. Tarcher/Putnam
a member of
Penguin Putnam Inc.
375 Hudson Street
New York, NY 10014
www.penguinputnam.com

Library of Congress Cataloging-in-Publication Data

Freed, Jennifer, date.
The ultimate personality guide / Jennifer Freed and Debra Birnbaum.
p.   cm.
ISBN 1-58542-070-0
1. Typology (Psychology).   2. Personality.   I. Birnbaum, Debra, date.   II. Title.
BF698.3.F74   2001   00-049099
155.2'6—dc21

Printed in the United States of America

1   3   5   7   9   10   8   6   4   2

Book design by Tanya Maiboroda

Contents

Acknowledgments

Though this book lists just two names as its creators, countless others had a hand (and a pen) in its production. First and foremost, we owe a tremendous thank-you to our editor, Wendy Hubbert, who had both the imagination to conceive of this book and the patience to see it through to its fruition. Simply put, this wouldn't exist if not for her efforts. Jennifer (Aquarius sun, Taurus moon, Sagittarius rising; rooster; Pitta; last-born) would like to thank Jennifer Louden for her expertise and faith; Dorothy Boswell for her symbolic imagination; Jan Scott and Candice Etz for their divine humor and wisdom; Carl Freed for his exquisite role as her brother; and Debra Birnbaum for her determination, skill, and grace. Last, Jennifer would like to express deepest gratitude to Rendy Freedman, who actually has the ultimate personality, and to the effervescent Nancy Freed, who invented the word "personality."

And Debra would like to thank her friends (Dawn, Rob, Lynne, and everyone at le shackteau) for their invaluable support and encouragement along the way—not to mention their willingness to be psychological guinea pigs. Thanks, too, to her sister, Jane, for being a firstborn who defies the rules (may Simon Levi break them all, too), and to Jennifer Freed, for her wisdom and stunningly accurate insight. Finally, a debt of gratitude is due to her parents, who not only laid the groundwork for their perfectionistic, Capricorn Kapha, but who also were never too shy to issue frequent, oh-so-subtle reminders about the status of "that book." *Todah rabah* to all of you.

The Ultimate Personality Guide

Introduction

*I*f we asked you to describe yourself, how would you begin? What words would you use? Most of us would probably turn first to physical characteristics: height, weight, hair and eye color. But while those qualities can go a long way in helping us each identify and recognize each other, they don't even scratch the surface of what's in someone's heart and soul. And that, in the end, is what really matters. Far more important than your physical traits are your personal and emotional ones: What are your likes and dislikes? Your strengths and weaknesses? Your secret dreams and fantasies? All of that is what makes us unique.

Experts of all kinds have developed typology systems to solve the riddle of personality. But the problem with most of these systems, such as astrology and numerology, is that they are too narrow in focus. They offer their own distinctive perspective on your personality, but don't allow for any individualistic traits that might not fit within the confines of that system. (Are all Leos really that self-centered? Are all youngest children rebellious?) In an effort to broaden that vision, some books have tried to combine personality systems: combining Chinese astrology with Western astrology, for example, or matching the enneagram with birth order. But this is somewhat like eating Thai food with Mexican food: it sounds like a great idea, but in the end, you're left with a soggy mess with no appealing flavor at all. In this book, for the first time, we have assembled the ultimate guide to truly understanding yourself and others.

We've given you the recipes for not just one or two but seven of the most widely used and highly respected personality systems in the world. We've boiled each down to the insightful wisdom each has to offer you; we'll leave it up to you to choose how many (or all, if you dare!) to take to heart. As you read each chapter—Western Astrology, Birth Order, Myers-Briggs–Inspired Typology, Enneagram, Ayurveda, Chinese Astrology, and Numerology—you'll be able to build a complete portrait of your personality: a 360-degree view of your potential in all areas of your life.

For each personality system, we'll explain the theories behind it and help you identify your type within that system. You'll learn what your strengths and weaknesses are, and how you can achieve more success and fulfillment in romance, friendship, health and fitness, career, and money. The more you understand yourself, the more you can improve your relationships with others. We'll give you hints on how to identify someone's type at first glance—and tips on which types make the best matches.

By the end of this book, you'll discover that it's not who you know or even what you know that matters—it's rather what you know about yourself that makes all the difference in life.

1

Western Astrology

*S*o, what's your sign?

Other than being the source of one of the worst pickup lines in the history of dating, astrology is also probably the best known of all the personality tests in our culture. Though skeptics may roll their eyes in disbelief, astrology has an intensely loyal following.

Humans have long looked to the stars for answers about life on earth. The study of astrology holds that the exact alignment of the sun, the moon, and the planets at the precise moment of your birth determines your true nature. Your future is up to you, astrologers say—but the stars have laid your path.

Astrology actually does have a basis in scientific principles about the relative position of the stars and the planets. We know that over the course of a year, the earth completes one revolution around the sun. Under the principles of astrology, that revolution is divided into twelve arcs of thirty degrees each. Each of those arcs is named for the constellation of stars that "rises" at that time (usually for a period of about thirty days). Most of those constellations (though not all) are named for animals—hence the term *zodiac*, which means "circus of animals" in Greek.

Welcome, then, to the most amazing show on earth—and sky.

What Sign Are You?

To get the most complete portrait of your astrological personality, it's important to know not only the date of your birth but also the exact time of your birth and place. Those three pieces of information will help you determine your sun sign (which shapes your basic identity and sense of self), your moon sign (your inner nature, your emotional reality, and your unconscious drives), and your rising sign (your social style, or how you come across to others).

Identifying your sun sign is simple—it's just a matter of the date of your birth (see chart below)—but you'll need to consult an astrologer to help you identify your moon and rising signs, because they're dependent on the time and place of your birth. (We just don't have the space here to include the charts for all possible combinations.) You can also visit www.yourastrologysite .com to get a copy of your complete birth chart.

Sun Signs

Aries: March 21–April 20
Taurus: April 21–May 20
Gemini: May 21–June 20
Cancer: June 21–July 22

Leo: *July 23–August 22*
Virgo: *August 23–September 22*
Libra: *September 23–October 22*
Scorpio: *October 23–November 21*
Sagittarius: *November 22–December 21*
Capricorn: *December 22–January 19*
Aquarius: *January 20–February 18*
Pisces: *February 19–March 20*

Aries
(THE RAM)
Ruling Element: Fire

Ariens are characterized by boundless courage, enthusiasm, and energy—but also impetuousness. You're driven by a need to achieve and be successful; you're the type to plow straight ahead to the heart of a problem and solve it while others stand by idly, twiddling their thumbs. Your instinctive determination to take charge makes you a self-assured, dynamic leader, but you're also prone to blindly stepping on a few toes along the way. You're so eager to get the job done that you tend to be somewhat impulsive and impatient, and your aggressiveness, though well intentioned, can rub others the wrong way. While others admire your drive and confidence, they may also perceive you as rather quick-tempered and reckless.

Strengths
Powerful, strong-willed, dramatic, outgoing, innovative, and assertive

Weaknesses

Selfish, rash, impulsive, demanding, tactless, insensitive, and hotheaded

Overall Self-improvement Goals

To learn to consider the needs of others with more compassion and grace, and to learn to share, both physically and emotionally

Your Love Life

Because they usually follow their hearts instead of their heads, Ariens fall in love at first sight—and fall hard, especially for people who are as lively and quick as they are. You can save yourself a lot of heartache by trying to be less hasty jumping into relationships. When do you find that special someone, make an effort to give more of yourself and open yourself up to intimacy, which can only strengthen the bond between you. It's important for Ariens to remember to look at any situation from their partners' point of view as well. The feelings of others are just as valid as yours.

Your Friendships

Ariens seek out friends who'll go along on whatever ride catches their eye. You've got little patience for doubters who sit on the sidelines debating whether or not to go ahead. But while your ideal friends are as action oriented as you are, they should also be a bit more refined and diplomatic, to help soften your rough, abrasive edges. You can be a better friend to them by trying to be less impulsive and more thoughtful. Try to remember that delayed gratification can still be immensely satisfying. And learn to be less quick to pass judgments on others. If you take the time to get to know someone, you may find that you have more in common than you think.

Your Career

Not surprisingly, Ariens are tremendously successful in the business world. Their competitive spirit and natural leadership skills will inevitably push them forward in whatever career they've chosen. As an Aries, you're a natural for fields that require a bit of daring, like police work, firefighting, or the military, as well as those that call for creative problem solving, like engineering. But as you plow ahead at work, take time to slow down and communicate more with both your colleagues and your superiors. Your tendency to be headstrong and self-involved may be holding you back from greater successes.

Your Finances

As an Aries, your sharp business sense has brought you financial rewards, but your aggressiveness may lead you to make foolish financial choices. Though most of the time these risks pay off for you, you do need a more cautious, balanced plan to assure your financial stability. Think about investing in mutual funds, which can offer you the excitement of the stock market with the stability of a more constant rate of return.

Health and Fitness

Ariens are the most robust athletes, thanks to their inexhaustible energy. You are jocks and muscle builders—but you've got big appetites, especially for spicy food, so you need plenty of exercise to keep in shape. Sports and activities that can expend a great deal of energy are your best bet—try tennis (singles, please—not doubles!), marathon running, and skiing. Be careful, though, to listen to your body's signals, and don't push yourself too hard. You're at risk for muscle strain if you don't take care to cool down. Try, too, to eat more vegetables instead of just protein-heavy meals, and drink plenty of water.

How to Recognize an Aries

You look fit and in charge, oozing confidence from head to toe. You've got a bold, elegant style sense; you dress in sleek, vibrant colors, and always have the perfect, eye-catching accessory.

Famous Ariens

Patricia Arquette, Alec Baldwin, Ellen Barkin, Warren Beatty, Mariah Carey, Tracy Chapman, Claire Danes, Celine Dion, Al Gore, Elton John, David Letterman, Rosie O'Donnell, Colin Powell, Paul Rudd, Emma Thompson, Steven Tyler, Reese Witherspoon

Taurus
(THE BULL)
Ruling Element: Earth

Those born under the sign of Taurus are represented by the bull, an animal known for its resolute stubbornness. It's your defining characteristic, in both positive and negative ways. At your best, you're determined, persistent, and enduring; you're a reliable, trusted ally. You like your way of doing things—you've been doing it that way for years, and wouldn't think of doing otherwise. You've set a steady routine in life; people could set a clock by you and your habits. But your stubbornness also means you're highly resistant to change. You tend to be inflexible in your habits and your beliefs, which others might find offputting.

Strengths

Placid, down-to-earth, patient, stable, stalwart, sensible, and charming

Weaknesses

Obstinate, stingy, overbearing, plodding, self-indulgent, possessive, materialistic, and conservative

Overall Self-improvement Goals

To set aside your need for constant security, and become more flexible, risk taking, and open to change

Your Love Life

Afraid of being hurt, you don't enter into relationships lightly, but because of your strong desire for emotional security when you do commit, you commit for life. As a result, you tend to hang on too long after a relationship has run its course. The biggest threat to your romantic happiness is your jealousy and possessiveness, which partners may find stifling. Learn to let go a little, and allow your mate some independence, which you could learn to enjoy, too. A breath or two of fresh air can only revitalize your relationship. You also tend to seek out relationships that can offer you security, but there needs to be passion in the mix as well. You're a sensual person; you deserve a lover who can ignite the smoldering flames within you.

Your Friendships

People are drawn to your common sense and natural charm. You're a loyal, true friend to those who can delve beneath your thick skin and draw you out. Especially in large social settings, you tend to be somewhat introverted, and something of a wallflower. Try to open yourself up to meeting new people and trusting them with your friendship.

Your Career

Methodical and responsible, you're a trusted worker and a key asset to your employer. You're ambitious, but you prefer working in a stable environment that guarantees you a steady paycheck. (No risky Internet start-ups for you, dear Taurus!) Fields like banking, insurance, finance, even the stock market—for a solid, blue-chip company, of course—will satisfy your need for security while rewarding you with the comfortable income you deserve for all your hard work. You might benefit, though, by being more free spirited and open-minded to new opportunities. Given your innate well groundedness, you're not likely to find yourself on the unemployment line.

Your Finances

Your need for security applies not only to your heart but also to your wallet. You've been accumulating wealth slowly but surely since your first allowance; you were never the type of kid to break into your piggy bank and splurge on the latest fad, and that constancy has followed you into adulthood. You don't need to be reminded that money can provide a secure future; that's why your finances are probably already in solid, long-term investments. You could be a little less, shall we say, attached to your funds (charity is always a good cause, and it's tax deductible), but otherwise, you're at the top of the financial astrological charts.

Health and Fitness

If money is your strength, then health and fitness is your weak spot. Tauruses often turn to food for the security they crave, and as a result, may overindulge and put on extra weight. You need to set up a program that will discipline your diet and exercise habits, and keep you from straying. Get your heart pumping with a regular schedule of aerobics, dancing, or jogging; and work salads and vegetables into your usual meat-eating routine.

How to Recognize a Taurus

Tauruses aspire to be like a regal bull—though without the nose ring (too daring!). You're known for your aesthetic, beautiful taste, and tend to dress in comforting, warm shades (blues and greens) in fabrics with texture, like velvet, silk, or linen.

Famous Tauruses

Andre Agassi, Bono, George Clooney, Pierce Brosnan, Daniel Day-Lewis, Billy Joel, Jessica Lange, Jay Leno, Ryan O'Neal, Jerry Seinfeld, Barbra Streisand, Uma Thurman, Renée Zell-weger

Gemini
(THE TWINS)
Ruling Element: Air

Like their namesake Twins, Geminis aren't easily pigeonholed. In fact, you resist being labeled at all costs. You're innately curious, and you love exploring and trying new things—often more than one at a time. A gifted, lively dilettante, you're always eager to learn a new skill, take on a new challenge, try a new restaurant. You're on a lifelong quest for constant stimulation, and you get bored easily. If you sit still for too long, if you feel you're not being challenged intellectually or physically, you get restless and impatient, and head for the door at the earliest opportunity. As a result, you don't take the time to get to know someone or something—which means some may call you superficial.

Strengths

Witty, versatile, entertaining, progressive, quick-witted, vivacious, inquisitive, and inventive

Weaknesses

Scattered, fickle, unpredictable, deceitful, and unreliable

Overall Self-improvement Goals

To learn to be in the moment and stay focused on the task at hand

Your Love Life

Because even you need a relationship that has some common ground, you should find an intellectually stimulating partner who shares some but not all of your interests and opinions. You need some discussion and argument to keep the passion alive; otherwise you'll be tempted to look outside the relationship time and again. You're an incurable flirt, and your partner will need to be understanding and forgiving of your wandering eye. But in turn, you must learn to be more constant and warmer, and to show your partner exactly how you're feeling. And stop flirting with every attractive stranger who catches your eye.

Your Friendships

Geminis are not lacking in friends; in fact, you're so gregarious and sociable that you're at the top of everyone's invitation list. You've got a well-connected, wide circle of friends who are thrilled to be in your company. But you may be lacking that one true soul mate to whom you can open your heart, because you're not willing to sit still long enough to do so. There is most likely someone in your life who is worthy of your friendship, and who cares enough about you to ride life's endless wave with you. In return, you need to give him or her your full attention when it's called for.

Your Career

Your quick wit and strong sense of logic serve you well at work. You're best suited for a job that makes the most of those skills, like journalism, writing, teaching, or the media. You also wouldn't mind a position that involves travel, such as sales, since you find any kind of routine suffocating. (Your gift of gab would come in handy with sales, too.) But you tend to get bored easily, especially if you're working alone, and you need work that's fast moving and changeable. Even in such a job, though, you must learn to be punctual, steady, and focused.

Your Finances

Because of your immeasurable talents, you've achieved a certain level of financial success, but money doesn't interest you per se. What does attract you is the ability to spend on a whim, to buy on impulse. Money to you is like candy—and you need to be careful of overindulging your sweet tooth. Ask a trusted financial advisor or accountant for help in setting up an untouchable candy jar, where you can keep your savings out of reach.

Health and Fitness

Your nervous Gemini energy helps keep you in shape; you never sit still long enough to overeat. Burn off some of that energy with squash, tennis, or jogging—and remember to get plenty of sleep so you can replenish your reservoir of energy. Long walks and gardening will also help ground you, as will a diet rich in root vegetables, like yams, potatoes, carrots, and beets.

How to Recognize a Gemini

Good luck trying to spot one: Geminis are those people flitting around a room, darting from place to place, rarely sitting still long enough to be noticed. You can't be bothered with frills and complicated fashions; you prefer to wear casual, comfortable clothes that allow you to chase every whim.

Famous Geminis

Rupert Everett, Michael J. Fox, Anne Heche, Angelina Jolie, Nicole Kidman, Helen Hunt, Elizabeth Hurley, Kristin Scott Thomas

Cancer
(THE CRAB)
Ruling Element: Water

Cancers are emotional, sensitive people. The most family oriented of all the signs, you crave loving, protective relationships that can shelter and nurture you. You offer plenty of warmth, caring, and empathy, but you can be so needy yourself that sometimes you may not be giving others their fair share of TLC. You're very thin-skinned, and so you take offense easily and may hold grudges for a long time; you don't easily forget slights against you. You've also got a tendency to be moody and withdrawn; when you're not happy or satisfied with the reality playing out in front of you, you simply shut down and shut yourself off.

Strengths

Affectionate, nurturing, compassionate, imaginative, intuitive, protective, and thoughtful

Weaknesses

Introverted, worrisome, clinging, withdrawn, overly cautious, unforgiving, and highly defensive

Overall Self-improvement Goals

To become more self-reliant and emotionally stable

Your Love Life

Cancers are true romantics, naturally caring partners who commit fully to every relationship and demand full commitment in return. As a Cancer, you're especially drawn to debonair, powerful people who you feel can protect you and help you build the home and family you want so deeply. But because of your sensitive nature, you're easily hurt and prone to fits of moodiness. In order to keep your relationships strong, you should try to be more direct with your partner. Be honest about your feelings, so others can be more aware of your points of fragility. But be careful, though, not to be too needy, which can turn some people off. Learn to stand on your own and find other sources of emotional support outside of your primary relationship.

Your Friendships

As with your romantic interests, you seek out friends who you feel worthy of your trust. But again, your neediness can be something of a turnoff, especially when you're too quick to take offense or harbor a grudge. Try to be less judgmental and more direct. If something is bothering you, resist your tendency to scramble into a hole and isolate yourself, which may confuse and distress your friends and others who care about you. Instead, tell someone close to you what's on your mind, what's hurting you. Trusting others to help you is beneficial for both you and them.

Your Career

Given a Cancer's limitless capacity for nurturing, you're ideally suited for caring professions, like health care or therapy. You're bound to feel fulfilled by helping others and soothing their problems—and you instinctively know how to do so. Be sure, though, to set boundaries; you don't want to be overwhelmed by other people's worries in addition to your own.

Your Finances

Money is an emotional issue—and emotions are your weakness. Some Cancers can be overly generous, equating money with love, while others can be withholding, clinging to money for security. The key words for your sign, then, are temperance and moderation. Whichever way your financial tendencies lie, try to keep your excessive habits in check and separate the dollar signs from your heartstrings.

Health and Fitness

As a Cancer, you've got a delicate constitution, which is ruled by your emotional nature. You're prone to stress-related illnesses and stomach problems, and may tend to emotional overeating. Your love of food may also predispose you to a certain degree of roundness. Regular rhythmic exercise like running, swimming, or dancing will help keep you in shape. And try to remember to eat for nutrition, not emotion.

How to Recognize a Cancer

Cancers exude warmth—they're the kind of people you want to run up to and hug. You opt for comfort over style; your clothes tend to drape your body rather than cling to it seductively.

Famous Cancers

Tom Cruise, John Cusack, Harrison Ford, Meryl Streep, Robin Williams, Carly Simon, Courtney Love, Tom Hanks, Anthony Edwards

Leo
(THE LION)
Ruling Element: Fire

The kings of the jungle—and the zodiac—Leos are powerful, flamboyant, confident personalities. Like the lion you're named for, you stride purposefully through life, with a trademark laser-beam focus on your next conquest. Failure is not an option, and any sign of weakness is simply unacceptable. You live to rule and to be admired for your many accomplishments. But your ruthless ambition, which has served you well on a personal level, has also won you many enemies. Your self-confidence can be perceived as haughtiness; your take-charge attitude tends to be somewhat abrasive and caustic. You're also a bit hot-tempered: When you're dissatisfied or disappointed in others, you've got quite an intimidating roar.

Strengths

Dignified, creative, exuberant, competitive, determined, charismatic, and individualistic

17

Weaknesses

Narcissistic, arrogant, intolerant, condescending, self-centered, conceited, pompous, and imperious

Overall Self-improvement Goals

To be more compassionate and sensitive to the needs and feelings of others

Your Love Life

Leos love being in love; the attention and flattery feeds their voracious egos. But you have to be careful about keeping the balance of power in check. With your need for constant reassurance, you're too quick to soak up all the praise and adoration without giving out much in return. And then you're left with a weakened, vulnerable partner whom you've suddenly lost interest in. Because you need someone who can keep up with you, be sure to give your partner space to be himself or herself. Learn to compromise, and try to be less overbearing and more attuned to your partner. Don't be so quick to grab the spotlight; and don't let pride come between you and your mate.

Your Friendships

Leos tend to treat people as subordinates rather than peers, which leaves them with few true friends who truly know their vulnerabilities. Opening up and sharing your innermost thoughts is not a sign of weakness; in fact, you find yourself relieved by the reassurance you receive in return. Share more, listen more, and give more—and you'll be rewarded with a trusted confidant you can turn to at all hours.

Your Career

Because of their innate powers of leadership, Leos often rise to the top of an organization or industry. You simply can't imagine not being the decision maker or being in the limelight. You might be a heart surgeon or even an actor. You've also got strong creative urges that can play out in your job—perhaps as a fashion designer or an artist—and you have a gift for the imaginative and the fantastic. You'll find even greater success, though, if you are more thoughtful, patient, and considerate of others along the way. You can't run your corporation alone.

Your Finances

Your ruthless ambition has, not surprisingly, brought you significant financial rewards. But you tend to treat money like a game, risking needlessly for the pure thrill of it. You appreciate the comfort and beauty that money affords you, but you need to learn the art of conservation and preservation in order to protect the lifestyle you enjoy so much.

Health and Fitness

As befits their stature in the animal kingdom, Leos have strong constitutions and are in fine physical condition. As a Leo, your best choices for exercise are activities where you can be seen— such as tennis, basketball, or other team sports—because your fuel is the adulation of others. Working with a personal trainer may also give you the admiration you seek. Living in a culture like ours that places such emphasis on body image, you're well aware of the impact of your diet on your figure. You may tend to overindulge in rich, creamy foods for the pleasure of it, but you're likely to rein in that habit naturally the second you stop getting admiring glances on the street.

How to Recognize a Leo

Leos are regal kings and queens—bejeweled and bewitching. You have a flamboyant, extravagant sense of style, and you use your wardrobe to make the most of what features you have to flaunt. You tend to dress in shades of deep purple and burgundy—the colors of luxury and royalty.

Famous Leos

Madonna, Ben Affleck, Robert De Niro, Whitney Houston, Jennifer Lopez, Sean Penn, Robert Redford, Kevin Spacey

Virgo
(THE VIRGIN)
Ruling Element: Earth

For better or worse, you're one of the few signs of the zodiac named not for an animal but for a character: the Virgin. Your sexual history notwithstanding, your sign has imbued you with a strong sense of duty and responsibility. You're quite practical in all matters; renowned for your common sense and unfailing tact and discretion, you're a wise, trusted advisor to friends and family. Where you falter is your level of adherence to what you consider proper. If pushed too far, you tend to be perfectionistic and overly critical. You're rather unforgiving of flaws in yourself and others; while others might laugh off mistakes, you can be humorless and judgmental.

Strengths

Practical, discerning, realistic, analytical, perceptive, and efficient

Weaknesses

Picky, conservative, fussy, and hypercritical

Overall Self-improvement Goals

To be more tolerant and learn to accept yourself and others for who they are, warts and all

Your Love Life

While others make their romantic missteps by blindly trusting their hearts, you shake your head in dismay. You let your mind lead you, analyzing and evaluating every potential romance from a distanced perspective. Rarely do you plunge ahead and invest your heart in anyone who doesn't meet your high standards. But in doing so, you deprive yourself of the incredible potential of passion, of true romance. Though you're a faithful partner once you do commit, you're still highly critical of yourself and your loved one, which can serve to widen the gap between you. A refined, nurturing partner may forgive you, but you should still try to be more generous and open-minded in return.

Your Friendships

Virgos are talkative, lively people, so you're a welcome addition to any social situation. But you do tend to hold your close friends to impossibly high standards, then cut them off coldly if they disappoint you (which they do, time and again). Artistic people might be more understanding of your perfectionism (they understand that artistic temperament of yours). Other characteristics of ideal friends for you are creativity, energy, and an ability to draw out your dormant sense of humor. Try to be more easygoing and forgiving of friends.

Your Career

Industrious to your core, you live for your work—especially if it taps into your skills of organization and precision. You'd enjoy work as a doctor, scientist, or engineer, especially since those fields call for a strict adherence to methodology. You might even make a good judge—though you'd definitely be prone to rendering harsher than average sentences. You can be a bit severe when it comes to judging others, so loosen up. Tell a funny story at the water cooler; forward a funny E-mail to some co-workers. The work will still get done—so would it hurt to smile, even just a bit?

Your Finances

You lie awake at night worrying about money—will you have enough for the mortgage, the tuition, the car payments? Of course you will—you're hardly the type to spend recklessly. You can be overly frugal with your money, afraid to spend lest you find yourself in some financial crisis someday, some year. Trust in your preference for safe investments, but don't hold yourself back from the occasional low-risk stock opportunity or small splurge on a guilty pleasure.

Health and Fitness

Virgos are prone to high levels of stress and tension, and their bodies suffer as a result. Holistic remedies like acupuncture and relaxation techniques like yoga are your best option for ridding your mind and body of toxins. Take a daily long walk to get fresh air; go for a slow-paced bike ride through the park. Your eating habits are probably beyond reproach—so treat yourself to that rich fudge brownie you've had your eye on.

How to Recognize a Virgo

With their penchant for cleanliness and tidiness (and even a dash of fastidiousness), Virgos tend to wear well-tailored, traditional clothing. Your style sense is simple, elegant, and classic—you're the one in the timeless black suit. Your understated wardrobe takes you from season to season, outlasting the in-one-day, out-the-next trends.

Famous Virgos

Sean Connery, Cameron Diaz, Richard Gere, Salma Hayek, Pee Wee Herman, Michael Jackson, Gwyneth Paltrow, Claudia Schiffer

Libra
(THE SCALES)
Ruling Element: Air

Alas, poor Libras: You're named not for an animal, but for a sterile piece of equipment: the Scales. Take heart, though—that means that you're the most balanced of all the signs. At least you strive to be. Your overall goal is for harmony in all areas of your life—in fact, you need harmony in order to be happy. With your cool, elegant, unflappable demeanor, you find it easily. You're an inveterate diplomat, able to see both sides of any situation. But in your attempts to always reach a fair, just decision, you tend to procrastinate for fear of making a foolish or hasty choice.

Strengths

Idealistic, peaceful, artistic, impartial, sophisticated, charming, sociable, and sympathetic

Weaknesses

Indecisive, dependent, self-indulgent, shallow, vain, and syco-phantic

Overall Self-improvement Goals

To become balanced without sacrificing personal values and to learn to abide by the choices you make

Your Love Life

A romantic to your core, you're happy only when you're in a re-lationship—you need the support of a partner so that you can feel balanced and complete. You may, though, take a while to commit fully, since you're so tortured by the process of making decisions. You're attracted to those who are ambitious, attractive, and who can offer you the emotional stability you crave. But don't expect your partner to be perfect, and don't bend over backward trying to please him or her at your own expense. If you're more truthful to yourself and less capricious, and if you and your partner are both more willing to explore each other's depths, you'll be able to build a fulfilling, mutually satisfying re-lationship.

Your Friendships

You may be tortured and indecisive when it comes to making your own life choices, but you're incredibly impartial and rea-sonable when it comes to helping others see clearly. Friends seek you out for your wise counsel and assistance in resolving their personal dilemmas. In turn, you need friends who are provoca-tive enough to inspire you to explore new challenges and experi-ences. People are drawn to your impeccable sense of style and glamour, but you need to be less catty and judgmental of others who don't meet with your approval. Don't be so quick to judge others on their surface appearance.

Your Career

You enjoy the high life, and so you need to earn good money to support the lifestyle you desire. You're well suited for the fashion and beauty industries, which allow you to express your artistic talents. You're also a skilled negotiator who could find great success in sales or the judiciary. You're likely to function best in a partnership; when working alone, you may lack patience or motivation.

Your Finances

You know the high price of your tastes, since you are prone to high spending and enjoy throwing your money around. But because you also tend toward balance, you're instinctively aware that you need to keep your financial spending in check. Libras should learn to save from a young age and to spread their investments out to ensure a balanced portfolio.

Health and Fitness

Libras love to be attractive, and they want to have bodies that others admire. So you know that you need to exercise, even though the thought of exertion and sweat is distasteful. You're most likely to enjoy exercise that feels good as well as looks good, such as yoga or skiing. Your diet, too, could be more balanced, since you have a weakness for rich, expensive foods. Control that desire with the occasional indulgence, but don't let overindulging overtake your meals.

How to Recognize a Libra

Appearances are important to Libras—you pride yourself on your sophisticated, elegant sense of style. You want to be in balance with your surroundings, so you always manage to find just the right thing to wear—never garish, never too revealing.

Famous Libras

Matt Damon, Jenna Elfman, Carrie Fisher, Heather Locklear, Tim Robbins, Susan Sarandon, Barbara Walters, Sigourney Weaver, Kate Winslet, Catherine Zeta-Jones

Scorpio
(THE SCORPION)
Ruling Element: Water

Scorpios are powerful, passionate people with strong, forceful, magnetic personalities. You're intensely emotional—with both highs and lows—and can explode in anger or dissolve in tears at the drop of a hat. You demand—and feed on—the attention of others; you cannot and will not be ignored. You've got a strong sense of purpose, and you stride confidently (and yes, even arrogantly) toward your goals. You like being the center of attention, and deeply resent it when others grab a bit of your spotlight. You can be extremely competitive, jealous, and vengeful.

Strengths

Penetrating, determined, incisive, sexy, supportive, committed, strong-willed, and self-reliant

Weaknesses

Possessive, secretive, obstinate, stagnating, obsessive, suspicious, and ruthless

Overall Self-improvement Goals

To be less jealous of others and to learn to trust

Your Love Life

Given your unquenchable thirst for attention, you're a demanding, intense lover. You're sexy and passionate, but also extremely jealous and possessive—and this has compromised many of your relationships in the past. You need a partner who is sympathetic to your high levels of energy and will meet your demands with warmth and empathy. If you let go of your need to control and learn to trust your partner, you'll find that a healthier, longer-lasting relationship awaits you.

Your Friendships

It's been difficult for you to find true friends, because most people are uncomfortable watching you hog the spotlight or seeing you seethe in envy if it happens to shine on them for even just a moment. But you do want to be able to share your life with others and you'd like to find people who can support you as you ride your emotional roller coaster. Your ideal friends are accomplished in their own right, loyal, and stimulating—they're not people you can steamroll.

Your Career

You're very ambitious, and completely devoted to making whatever sacrifices necessary to get ahead. Where others would crack under pressure, you thrive. You love competitive, high-stress working environments, so you're an ideal stockbroker, surgeon, or detective (your insatiable need to know leads you to investigative occupations). Since you've probably already achieved tremendous success in your field, the main career challenge for Scorpios is to be more easygoing and relaxed. Your blood pressure could use the break.

Your Finances

You've got the intuition and inborn savvy for making money, and you realized early on that money paves the road to all the things you desire in life. Scorpios can be unstoppably successful, but they can also be equally self-destructive, using money as a weapon. You need to learn to view money as a means to an end, and not as a tool to win at all costs. Don't be tempted to use money to win your way with others. Remember, the stock market could come crashing down, and then you'll be looking for handouts, too.

Health and Fitness

It's feast or famine for you—you either exercise religiously or not at all. Either you control every morsel you put into your mouth, or you binge on your latest craving of choice. Given your emotional nature, moderation is the key word here, in both diet and exercise. Sports like swimming or martial arts will help keep you in shape while keeping your blood pressure level.

How to Recognize a Scorpio

You're sexy and you know it—and your clothes announce (in fact, scream) it to everyone you see. It's not that you bare cleavage or your rock-hard abs, but rather that you flaunt your assets. Your clothes—usually in dark, nearly monochromatic shades of purple, burgundy, and black—hug your body and flatter your figure. You're not afraid to stand out in a crowd.

Famous Scorpios

Whoopi Goldberg, Dennis Miller, Julia Roberts, Meg Ryan, Winona Ryder, Jodie Foster, Goldie Hawn, Ethan Hawke, Kevin Kline

Sagittarius
(THE ARCHER)
Ruling Element: Fire

Sagittarians are generally cheerful, highly energetic people. You love your freedom and the liberty to pursue your every whim; you're so innately restless, it's hard to tie you down and pin you in the moment. You thrive on having many interests and doing many things at once; challenge is important to you. In your overexuberance, however, you can be somewhat tactless and insensitive. You may be so caught up in your frenzy that you forget to consider the needs and feelings of others, even those closest to you.

Strengths

Enthusiastic, optimistic, open-minded, sociable, adventurous, gregarious, philosophical, and good-humored

Weaknesses

Superficial, garrulous, restless, phony, preachy, risk taking, foolhardy, and impulsive

Overall Self-improvement Goals

To learn to be more subtle, humble, and tactful

Your Love Life

Pity those who try to get a Sagittarius to commit or settle down: you value your freedom intensely and hate to be tied down; you're deathly afraid of feeling possessive or being possessed. A patient partner can tame your restlessness, win your trust, and teach you the benefits of true intimacy and connection, but you need to allow your mate to do so. Learn to listen and wait and share your soul with another—and let your partner reveal himself or herself to you.

Your Friendships

You're a classic extrovert. Your infectious good nature has brought you a wide circle of friends of many cultures and diverse interests. You thrive on having so many people surround you; they feed your ego and make you feel complete and free. Your friends enjoy your company—even if they only get your attention for a few minutes—because you're fun to be around. That is, except when you needlessly voice the unspeakable. Try to bite your tongue and not always say what's on your mind. Be more discriminating in expressing your feelings—your friends will be grateful.

Your Career

You don't like being pinned down behind a desk in a job that's going nowhere. You need a challenging job that makes use of your boundless energy. Try public relations, religion, teaching, or fund-raising—fields that allow you to interact with large groups of diverse people who will respond to your enthusiasm. In any position, though, you do have to learn to pay more attention to critical details, which often slip below your radar screen as you go on your endless pursuit of loftier goals.

Your Finances

You've never sat down long enough to do something as mundane as balance your checkbook—you just breezily assume you have the cash to pursue each of your whims as they come up. Fortunately, so far you've been very lucky financially; people respond to your warmth and energy, and you've been amply rewarded for your work. You have a weakness for risk taking and gambling, and may push your luck too far at the card tables or the slot machine. Rather than quash that gambling spirit—since it has probably brought you some financial reward—make sure you've got an inviolable piggy bank or money market account set up. The day may indeed come when you'll want to (gasp) settle down.

Health and Fitness

You're very sporty and athletic, with tremendous enthusiasm for outdoor activities and robust meals. But as we all get older, our metabolism slows regardless of level of exertion. So Sagittarians may become overweight if they keep up the thoughtless eating habits they tend to have. Rather than cut yourself off entirely from the foods you love, be sure to include challenging workouts as a key part of your daily routine. You won't feel restricted, since you enjoy physical activity, but the workouts will allow you the freedom to indulge a little.

How to Recognize a Sagittarius

You dress with an eye toward simplicity and comfort while adhering to style. Think blue jeans, with a simple sweater or twinset (you can't be bothered with fussy, frilly pieces), accessorized with a great pair of shoes or belt. You're especially drawn to shades of purple.

Famous Sagittarians

Woody Allen, John Malkovich, Bette Midler, Brad Pitt, Sting, Ben Stiller, Kim Basinger, Brendan Fraser, Kenneth Branagh, Steven Spielberg

Capricorn
(THE GOAT)
Ruling Element: Earth

Capricorns are responsible, reliable hard workers—the kind you always want on your team. A Capricorn will go to all lengths to get the job done and get it done right. In fact, you don't know any other way of doing it; you can't imagine leaving a project half-finished, even if it means staying up all night. Though your determination is admirable, it can also be your biggest downfall when it translates into stubbornness and rigidity. Put down the Filofax or Palm Pilot, and let yourself enjoy a few minutes of free time. You need to learn to let your hair down and laugh at your foibles instead of taking life so seriously.

Strengths
Disciplined, dependable, determined, honest, practical, and methodical

Weaknesses
Rigid, pessimistic, stubborn, aloof, blunt, and old-fashioned

Overall Self-improvement Goals
To become more lighthearted, to be more sensitive to the foibles of others, and to learn to share your knowledge with others

Your Love Life

Though you're a sensitive, emotional person, you've tended to put your work ahead of your emotional needs, and as a result, your love life has suffered for it. You tend to be somewhat calculating in seeking out partners who can offer you the status you crave without paying attention to whether they are emotionally compatible with you. Instead, be sure that your potential partners are not only well established in terms of career and finance but also good-natured and sensitive to your needs. You tend to be pretty critical of others, so try to be more appreciative and accommodating. And allow yourself to play. Work is, of course, important, but every now and then you need to get up from your desk and show affection to those you love. Capricorns can be emotionally reserved, but you'll get more love from your partner if you remember to tell him or her how much you care.

Your Friendships

You're a true friend because you're so reliable; you've never let anyone down. But you tend to make friends based on superficialities: your unquenchable thirst for status attracts you to the in crowd, and you're happiest when you're surrounded by accomplished and influential people. Try to learn to value others for the quality of their soul instead of the contents of their wallet. You can make yourself be a better friend by becoming more genuine and emotionally available, especially during the hard times—when your true, loyal character will come through.

Your Career

Here is where Capricorns shine. Driven by your ambition and need for success, you've been steadily climbing your way up the ladder, which has brought you considerable power, money, and prestige. You're an ideal leader or manager, who'll do well in careers in government, banking, or finance—or in your own field of entrepreneurship. You pride yourself on being a self-made success story. Though you enjoy working alone (in fact, you prefer it, because that way you're not subject to anyone else's failings), you do need to learn to play well with others, to strive for quality as well as status, and to slow down. You win when everyone else wins, too.

Your Finances

Your bank accounts reflect the fruits of your labor; your industriousness translates into a healthy portfolio. You're an instinctive saver, who'd shudder at the thought of squandering money on high-risk schemes. Instead, your funds are safely ensconced in safe, trusted stocks. You do tend, however, to be a bit too thrifty with your money. (You could probably recite the exact contents of your wallet right now, to the penny.) Critics might call you miserly and grudging. Remember to give to others in order to boost your spiritual health.

Health and Fitness

Your strongest assets are of the mental variety, not the physical. You're more likely to prefer sitting on the couch with a book to sitting on the exercise bicycle, but you do need to get regular exercise—both for your long-term physical health and because you are prone to depression, and regular movement and activity can help chase away the blues. Try walking or golf; though low impact, these activities are moderately aerobic. Your emotional health also affects the way you eat; you tend to use food for comfort when life gets too stressful. Instead, try to take more time for meals and eat slowly. You'll be more likely to eat healthfully if you actually taste what you're eating, instead of inhaling food at the rapid pace at which you tend to do most other things.

How to Recognize a Capricorn

Slaves to convention, Capricorns are very image conscious, and their clothing reflects it. While you're not one to take fashion risks, your clothes are expensive, distinctive, and distinguished, and designed for maximum comfort. Think cashmere, classic styles, even vintage.

Famous Capricorns

Anthony Hopkins, Val Kilmer, Diana Ross, Kirstie Alley, Katie Couric, Kate Moss, Julia Louis-Dreyfus, Nicolas Cage, Ricky Martin, Kevin Costner, Cuba Gooding, Jr., Jim Carrey, Ralph Fiennes, Mel Gibson, Jude Law, Tracey Ullman, Denzel Washington

Aquarius
(THE WATER BEARER)
Ruling Element: Air

Aquarians are known for being highly independent, for living by their own rules. At best, you're unconventional; at worst, eccentric. Your driving need for independence and the freedom to pursue your own fantasies and challenge the norm has made you quite rebellious and resistant of authority. As a result, you're extraordinarily creative and inventive—an ingenious thinker and innovator. But you tend to be so focused on your ideas and thoughts that you push aside others; you forget to open up and share your warmth and heart with the important people in your life.

Strengths

Independent, idealistic, intuitive, lively, altruistic, original, and inventive

Weaknesses

Prideful, cool, aloof, unemotional, contrary, unpredictable, and defensive

Overall Self-improvement Goals

To warm up to others, to learn to apologize, and not to be afraid of sharing your feelings

Your Love Life

You find it difficult to sustain relationships because it may mean putting another's needs ahead of your own. You have a hard time making a commitment; you run hot and cold as your attention to another person waxes and wanes. Your best matches are with those whom you perceive as exciting and unusual, though you're often guilty of being too detached, because you don't share feelings easily. Deep down you are a good, caring partner; so be sure to show it to your partner with displays of your feelings.

Your Friendships

You desire friends who are just like you—eccentric bohemians who thumb their noses at the status quo, and don't look down on you for doing the same. You and your friends are likely to challenge each other in your searches for the next big idea. But you should also go beneath the surface and open up your heart more to these friends by being more reliable, steady, and considerate of them. You have a tendency to pull away from others and shut yourself off unexpectedly, so you can be a better friend by being more constant—and especially letting friends know when you're feeling hurt.

Your Career

With your natural talent for innovative thinking, you're a natural scientist, inventor, or social reformer. Your innate flair and originality also mean that you have a keen sense of drama and a talent for the arts, like filmmaking, which tends, in your hands, to be cutting-edge. You want to change the world, but you'll find that it's easier to do so in tiny steps instead of huge leaps. If you stay focused on your work, your ideas will have a better chance of being realized.

Your Finances

Money? Aquarians can't be bothered. You hardly need it to maintain your bohemian lifestyle. But like all of us, you will need a solid nest egg someday, and so you should enlist the help of a good money manager to keep your grand visions firmly funded. Put the money you make from your creations into secure accounts that you can live off in those rare days of inventor's block.

Health and Fitness

Sweaty, aerobic exercise is too mundane a concept for you. Instead, you should try regular creative exercise like dancing, yoga, or walking to boost your circulation and maintain your metabolism. You probably need to be reminded to eat, because your thoughts are usually on a loftier plane. Light, small meals are your best bet to keep you fueled.

How to Recognize an Aquarius

You're an individual, and you dress to prove it. Your strong need to express your personality shows in your wardrobe, which is quirky and unique, yet also trend-setting. Your taste is innovative, and highly personalized, and you're especially drawn to energetic bright colors.

Famous Aquarians

Jennifer Aniston, Christie Brinkley, Phil Collins, Ellen De-Generes, Minnie Driver, Michael Jordan, Jennifer Jason Leigh, John McEnroe, Sarah McLachlan, Nick Nolte, Christina Ricci, Jane Seymour, Oprah Winfrey

Pisces
(THE FISH)
Ruling Element: Water

Pisces swim contentedly through the seas of life. You're an idealistic, creative dreamer; a sensitive, imaginative thinker who enjoys floating peacefully through the days. You dislike stirring up trouble—in fact, your weak spot is that you're too intent on pleasing others, and you can be too easily persuaded by them, at a cost to your own true self.

Strengths

Sensitive, compassionate, poetic, intuitive, dreamy, romantic, sensual, tender, and softhearted

Weaknesses

Delusional, reclusive, introverted, passive, impressionable, escapist, hapless, weak-willed, and martyrlike

Overall Self-improvement Goals

To take off your rose-colored glasses and learn to stand on your own two fins—er, feet

Your Love Life

A sensitive and romantic soul, you tend to fall in love blindly, head over heels, time and again. You're terribly afraid of being lonely, and so you'll tolerate far more than you should in others rather than risk being abandoned by them. You'll deceive yourself about your partner's flaws, telling yourself that those foibles don't really matter—when they do. You need a responsible partner who won't take advantage of you, and you, in turn, should be more detail oriented, more accountable to the work of building a relationship, because you're too quick to be swayed by emotion. Don't always follow your heart so blindly; think things through before you take huge leaps.

Your Friendships

Pisces are great friends because they're so selfless; they'll do anything for a friend. As a Pisces, your best friends are those who share your artistic spirit, but who are also practical and capable to help ground you, since you tend to be so ethereal. Despite your outward sensitivity, you tend to be evasive about sharing your inner emotions, reluctant to express clearly what you're really feeling. Your friends will get tired of this act quickly: in order to sustain long-term friendships, you must try to be more direct.

Your Career

Your love of beauty and the arts draws you to fields that allow you to be creative and immerse yourself in fantasy: film, music, poetry, philosophy. Because of your deep, emotional sensitivity, you'd be a wonderful counselor or psychologist, able to empathize with all who come to you. But you have to remember that the reason you work is to provide for your physical and emotional needs; you need that salary to support your lifestyle and your artistic visions. When it comes to work, you need to be more reliable and grounded. Keep regular office hours (well, as regular as a Pisces can), and try to get a steady job to pay the bills. And when it comes to collecting fees for your own efforts, don't let others push you around or your business ventures will suffer.

Your Finances

Pisces can be the richest of all signs as well as the poorest. You often make piles of money because of your talented creative impulses, but then you can lose the cash just as easily in pursuit of a whim. You've been conned out of money time and again by false advisors whose promises you accept blindly at face value. You're best advised to let your money grow safely in a money market account, or let a reliable broker make your investment decisions for you.

Health and Fitness

You're prone to worry and depression, which takes a toll on your digestive system and emotional health. A regular workout is key to your overall well-being; you need to find a routine (try tai chi or yoga) and stick to it. Not only will such activities keep you in good shape physically but they will help clear all the cobwebs from gathering in your head. Stress may also lead you to overeat and drink, so watch out for bingeing during moments of high (or low) emotion.

How to Recognize a Pisces

Pisces are dreamy looking, with their heads in the clouds. You tend to dress in colors of water—you're often seen in aquas, blues, greens.

Famous Pisces

Juliette Binoche, Chelsea Clinton, Cindy Crawford, Michael Eisner, Kelsey Grammer, Ron Howard, Spike Lee, Liza Minnelli, Sharon Stone, Bruce Willis

2

Birth Order

Remember *The Brady Bunch*? If you were a fan of the show, you probably had a favorite character. Was it Marcia, Jan, or Cindy Brady? (Or, for that matter, Greg, Peter, or Bobby?) The answer probably has less to do with your fondness for classic '70s sitcoms than with your relationship with your own family. Your sympathies probably lay with the Brady kid with whom you share birth-order position. Though it's simply a matter of fate and timing, our birth-order position—firstborn, middle, last, or only—is said by psychologists to have clear-cut, lasting effects on our personalities. (Of course, genetics, education, and life experiences also shape the adult we've become.)

Why do psychologists believe birth order has a powerful effect on our personalities? Intentionally or not, we defined ourselves during childhood in relation to our siblings—as did our parents. One child was the smart one; the other, the pretty one. One was artistic; the other athletic. Now consider those labels in the context of when you arrived in the family. As we were growing up with our siblings, we competed with each other to get our perceived fair share of our parents' attention (or lack thereof). How we fit in the birth order determined how we went about getting it. Firstborns, for example, had their parents all to themselves to fawn over their every first step—that is, until the new baby arrived. Suddenly they had to compete to get noticed. And indeed, as adults, firstborns tend to be competitive high achievers—the ranks of CEOs and company presidents teem with firstborns.

Countless studies have been performed in recent years supporting this personality theory. More often than not, the basic stereotypes that come to mind for each birth-order position do tend to be true: there's the assertive, dominant firstborn; the frustrated middle child, desperate to be noticed; and the spoiled baby who gets away with anything. Though formed in childhood, these behavior patterns—positive and negative, strong and weak—tend to follow us into our adult lives, like it or not.

Firstborns

The first to come into the family, firstborns basked in their parents' attention. You never had to share your parents with anyone else or cope with hand-me-downs. You were closely supervised, your every move celebrated—and, in all likelihood, photographed endlessly. You thrived in your parents' joy and devotion, but you alone also had to fulfill your parents' high expectations. You were probably pushed to walk, talk, and read at an early age.

And then your siblings started arriving. Whether the intruders arrived nine months or nine years later, you found yourself sent off on your own, forced to grow up independently a little too quickly. Attention could no longer be paid to *your* every move, because your young siblings were so much needier. So you became self-reliant, determined, and focused on your own success.

Firstborns usually walk and talk earlier and perform better at school. You're the "alpha males and females" of the family. Because you grew up bigger, stronger, and smarter than your siblings, as adults, you tend to be more assertive and dominant than your peers. You're therefore natural leaders, used to leading a gang of younger siblings, and even being surrogate parents for them. You're adept at rallying the troops around you. Here's a little-known but telling fact: twenty-one of the first twenty-three astronauts were the eldest children in their families (as is every actor who has played James Bond, for whatever that's worth). After all, being an astronaut *is* a job that requires tremendous self-confidence, independence, and innovation—all hallmarks of firstborns.

Because you were the guinea pigs on which your parents practiced laying down their laws, you have a tremendous respect for authority. You're closely wedded to your parents' standards and values, and therefore tend to be conservative. You also tend to be jealous of others, in work and in relationships, having experienced, early on, the invasion of your turf by unwelcome newcomers.

Strengths

Competitive, assertive, meticulous, and responsible

Weaknesses

Authoritarian, perfectionistic, critical, self-conscious, and self-righteous

Overall Self-improvement Goals

To learn to let go, relax, and find the fun in all that you do—
even (and especially) the hard work

Romance

You tend to be possessive of the things you own and the people
in your lives, probably because as a child you'd had to share with
your grabbing, demanding younger siblings—which made you
hold tightly on to whatever you could claim as your own. When
it comes to love, you need to learn to let go, to be more spontaneous. Because you're so focused on doing things your way, a relationship with a spontaneous, playful, creative, generous lover
will help you to grow as an individual. You need to learn to be
less nitpicky, and to lower your standards of performance and
expectation: your high standards can make it difficult for you to
be satisfied with your partners and relationships. When it comes
to romance, remember that not everything has to go by the rules.
You'll make yourself—and your partner—happier if you learn
to relax.

Friendship

Firstborns are loyal, responsible friends—you'll support your
buddies to the end. You seek out friends who are dependable, reliable, and open, because you don't want to be let down by those
you confide in. Your friendships would be even stronger, though,
if you learned to give your friends more latitude. Strive to be less
status conscious in your everyday life, and share more of your
own vulnerability with those who have placed their trust in you.

Work

Not surprisingly, a large proportion of politicians, chief executives, doctors, and lawyers are firstborns. Natural leaders, first-

borns are also the control freaks, the organization nuts. First-borns thrive in careers like architecture and accounting—anything that requires attention to detail. To reach your full potential, you should try to be less rigid. You tend to be closed to new ways of thinking, and may be slow to change even when your business calls for it. Try to open up to change and devote more attention to preserving and maintaining relationships at work. Make an effort to be less anxious about punctuality, fastidiousness, and the occasional mistake. Such behavior won't win you any friends, and you may make yourself sick from the stress.

Money

Firstborns are thrifty, economical, and shrewd about making money. But you're prone to becoming obsessive about it and pre-occupied with every little financial detail. If you want to enjoy the fruits of your labor, try to let go of your Scrooge tendencies and learn to enjoy the pleasures that money provides—like time to enjoy relationships, entertainment, and leisure.

Health and Fitness

As in other areas of life, firstborns tend to be driven when it comes to health and fitness. You'll run a marathon every week, or go to aerobics classes five times a day—pushing your body to suit some always-unattainable image of perfection. Come up with a reasonable (the key word here is *reasonable*) fitness plan that accentuates the process, not the product. Team sports are ideal for the firstborn, especially those that emphasize cooperation and enjoyment over competition and triumph. (Your competitive urges are probably satisfied already through your work.) As far as diet, try to let go of your obsessive control issues and stop treating your body like a machine.

How to Recognize a Firstborn

Firstborns tend to be pressed and ready to impress in their Armani or Calvin Klein suits. You carry yourself as a dignitary, no matter what hour of the day.

Famous Firstborns

Hillary Rodham Clinton, Nicole Kidman, Steffi Graf, Janet Reno, Katharine Hepburn, Dan Rather, Clint Eastwood, Shania Twain

Middle-Borns

Sandwiched between bossy, driven, older siblings and rebellious younger siblings, middle-borns usually assume the role of the family mediator and peacemaker. They're masterful diplomats, always concerned with making sure everyone's getting along.

But your flexibility comes at a high personal price. Middle-borns often feel lost and invisible, pushed out of the spotlight by your more demanding brothers and sisters. It's true that you've gotten a pretty raw deal: born too late to get all the attention lavished on the oldest, and born too soon to enjoy the freedom awarded to the youngest. Middle-borns will complain privately about getting the short end of the stick. But you're too eager to keep the peace to do anything about it—even at the price of your own self-esteem. Instead, you find your value and self-worth in needing to be needed.

Strengths

Even tempered, diplomatic, generous, easy to get along with, and open-minded. Middle-borns are great compromisers and negotiators.

Weaknesses

Inconsistent, wishy-washy, secretive, and overly conciliatory. Middle-borns prove that it *is* possible to be too accommodating.

Overall Self-improvement Goals

To be more direct in asking for positive attention instead of waiting for it to come to you

Romance

Given the middle-born's need to be needed, you tend to seek out partners with a yen to be controlled and possessed. But that doesn't necessarily always serve you well, because you're simply repeating the patterns of your childhood. Instead, you should find a partner who can stand on his or her own, while still relying on you for some emotional support. To be a better partner yourself, make an effort to be more assertive about your own needs. Otherwise, your unspoken resentments may undermine your mutual long-term happiness.

Friendship

As experienced peacemakers, middle children make loyal, faithful friends. But you should be careful not to go overboard in serving your friends at the expense of yourself. You need friends who won't take advantage of you, who will be sure to elicit your opinions and preferences. And you shouldn't be afraid of standing up for yourself, even if it means occasionally rocking the boat.

Work

The skills of middle-borns translate well to the workplace. You make good managers, because you know how to listen to all sides and work for the common good. You can size up any situation and know how to run for the touchdown, because you make a point of knowing all the players and their individual strengths and weaknesses. After all, that's what you've been doing in your family for years. Middle-borns are well suited for careers in advertising, sales, or any field that involves negotiating. To be a better worker, learn to delegate instead of carrying all the responsibility on your shoulders.

Money

Middle children often fall prey to the disease of impressiveness. Having been raised in the shadow of your siblings, you want to do more than keep up with the Joneses—you want to stand out! This often leads to spending beyond your means, so you'd be well served by soliciting professional assistance in devising a solid financial plan—and abiding by it.

Health and Fitness

Middle children have to be careful they don't grow a middle themselves. You're people pleasers who hardly say no to anything, so you often feed yourself more than you need. To maintain your ideal body weight, you need to be far more discriminating about the quantity and substance of your diet. You needn't finish everything on your plate simply because it's placed in front of you. Given your learned ability to work well with others, you're a great team player. To help you stick with a workout regimen, find a workout buddy who'll motivate you to go to the gym. When you were growing up, you probably pushed yourself to excel in a sport as a way to get noticed—a fine practice to continue into adulthood.

How to Recognize a Middle-Born

Blending into the crowd is a middle-born's worst nightmare. You will try anything—a revealing dress, a bold hairstyle—to stand out and gain attention for yourself. (Who can forget Jan Brady's experiment with the black curly wig?)

Famous Middle-Borns

Tim Allen, Julia Roberts, Ted Kennedy, Donald Trump, Rosie O'Donnell, Kim Basinger

Last-Borns

No matter how many children there are in a family, by the time the youngest arrives, all hell has probably broken loose within the family structure. The ideals with which your parents raised your elder siblings have long since been shattered, replaced with more realistic and flexible standards. The family's copy of Dr. Spock's book is probably tattered and torn, no longer the pristine bible it was when the firstborn arrived. And so you, the last-born, grew up with less respect for status quo and authority. Last-borns tend to be more daring, more risk taking, and far more liberal than firstborns. You're more open to new ways of thinking and doing things, whether or not those plans ever work out.

But being the last ones to the party, you also faced a struggle to find a niche for yourself, since your brothers and sisters had long since carved out their own roles. Since your older siblings absorbed most of the traditional pressure to succeed from your parents, many last-borns turn to creativity, independence, even rebelliousness to stand apart from their siblings. You're the clowns, the inventors, the revolutionaries, the rebels of the family—the ones most likely to make your parents shrug their shoulders in helplessness. Much to the chagrin of your older siblings, your parents were likely to have been far more lax with you. Your brothers and sisters probably spent a lot of time complaining—and still do—that you, the baby of the family, were spoiled and indulged, and got away with (relative) murder.

Strengths

Outgoing, sociable, affectionate, and creative

Weaknesses

Spoiled, manipulative, self-centered, and capricious. Last-borns need to be the center of attention at all times, and you are often guilty of avoiding taking responsibility for your actions.

Overall Self-improvement Goals

To bring a more committed approach to all that you do, by following through on any and all promises you make

Romance

Because of your tendency toward flightiness, you are best paired with partners who are mature and stable, who have the intelligence and power to ground you and bring you back to earth. Because your parents may have spoiled you as a child, you can work on being a better partner by being more considerate, responsible, and picking up after yourself—in all respects.

Friendship

Sociable and popular, the life of every party you attend, you usually have a wide circle of friends who are willing to give you full and devoted attention. To be a better friend yourself, try to give others as much attention as you demand from them. Start by listening, instead of talking.

Work

Firstborns may make for the best executives, but last-borns are the trailblazers and innovators of the business world. Last-borns are often successful entrepreneurs as well as artists and inventors. You thrive in careers that offer a sense of freedom and enough independence so that you can produce according to your talents. Last-borns do tend to be overly excitable, though, which makes you hard to work with. Make an effort to be more even tempered, and learn to share the limelight with others.

Money

Last-borns can be far too frivolous with money. Your bank accounts are constantly tapped, since you spend every cent as quickly as you earn it, and will eagerly plunge your entire net worth into any risky venture that catches your attention. You need to learn the value of conservation and saving; even a basic money market account is a step in the right direction. You would also be well served by seeking out an investment advisor who can monitor your money and make sound financial decisions for you.

Health and Fitness

You get excited about athletics when you get a good dose of mirroring—meaning that you get attention for what you're doing from others who are watching and cheering you on. You hunger to be the star of the team, the one who gets the kudos and ovations. In order to continue being part of that successful team, though, you should learn to share the spotlight, to take part in athletic activities where *all* can succeed and benefit. As for your diet, last-borns are instant-gratification junkies. You have a great appetite for the intense, gustatory experience, which unfortunately brings with it a potential for gluttony. Be especially careful about overindulging your whims.

How to Recognize a Last-Born

It's not hard to spot a last-born—you *want* to be recognized, to stand out. You're likely to wear the unconventional and the shocking simply to get a reaction out of people. Green hair, numerous body piercings, skintight leather pants—classic signs of the rebellious last-born.

Famous Last-Borns

Howard Stern, Gloria Steinem, Bill Gates, Jodie Foster, Ralph Nader, Anita Hill, Danny DeVito, Jay Leno, Ashley Judd

Only Children

To understand only children, think of them as firstborns—and then throw some extra perfectionism in for good measure. As an only, you wallowed in your parents' undivided attention for your *entire* childhood. You never had to fight for your share of the pie; you always got as much as you wanted. You were the precocious kid who was always comfortable in a roomful of adults, and so as an adult, you exude self-confidence. But because you alone had to live up to your parents' standards, you tended to set high, often unattainable standards for yourself and others. As a result, onlies often push people away by being overly critical and demanding. It's ironic, because you want nothing more than to be loved and included; your greatest fear is of being alone as you were as a child. Onlies are hard to get to know on a personal level, since you've got a tough outer shell, but inside, you're deeply nurturing and supportive, enriched by all the love you received growing up.

Strengths

Self-assured, detail oriented, self-motivated, and ambitious

Weaknesses

Self-centered, spoiled, unyielding, high-strung, and overly analytical

Overall Self-improvement Goals

To become more spontaneous and to not take life so seriously. If you want to be included, you need to learn the benefits of sharing with others—a lesson you probably didn't practice much as a child.

Romance

Ideal partners are those who can admire and appreciate you while helping you loosen up and enjoy yourself. You can be a better partner yourself by always checking to see if you've considered your partner's needs before your own—since you're often guilty of the crime of looking out for number one to the exclusion of anyone else.

Friendship

Onlies are prone to feeling lonely—a lingering remnant of your solitary childhood. So you need just a close friend or two who are generous and good-natured and can take your stubbornness in stride. You'll be a better friend if you remember to be more open-minded and to accept people as they are, flaws and all.

Work

Onlies will thrive in careers that utilize all their intellectual and emotional muscle, such as nuclear engineer, physicist, or president of a bank. You enjoy challenging work with an active pace, and though you are highly productive, you have a tendency to drive yourself and others too hard. By focusing too much on the outcome, you tend to ignore the process, and you can thereby alienate co-workers and subordinates. To build stronger relationships in the workplace and foster harmony, you need to learn to share tasks and credit with colleagues, subordinates, and supervisors.

Money

Given their high regard for achievement and unforgiving drive, onlies are great wage earners. You probably find great security in the size of your bank accounts, but you have a tendency toward hoarding, and you need to learn the joy of sharing your wealth with others through thoughtful gifts and charitable donations. You may also need to remind yourself to lighten up and splurge once in a while. You deserve it.

Health and Fitness

Rarely is diet and exercise a trouble spot for onlies—you're usually very active and fit because of the high standards to which you hold yourself. If anything, you need to learn to take on less and to work with your body in a kinder manner. Make an effort to participate in exercises oriented toward enjoyment and fun as goals instead of competition—a game of beach volleyball, a friendly touch football game in the park. There's no need to fuel your already overly competitive instincts. As for diet, you need to be mindful of when and what you're eating, given your proclivity to do everything at a fast pace. If you eat too quickly and mindlessly, you may not be eating healthfully and getting all the nutrients you need. A little preplanning of your daily menu will ensure that you have a well-rounded, nutritionally complete diet.

How to Recognize Onlies

With your impeccably coiffed and tastefully fashionable appearance, you grab attention and admiring glances everywhere you go.

Famous Onlies

Ted Koppel, Dick Cavett, Nancy Reagan, Carol Burnett, Joe Montana, Chelsea Clinton, Jennifer Aniston, Oprah Winfrey

Best and Worst Matches

Best Matches

℮ Firstborn with last-born: Like a jigsaw puzzle, you balance out the other's weaknesses.

℮ Only with middle-born: One is needy, the other needs to be needed. While one is demanding attention, the other can be conciliatory and keeping the peace.

Worst Matches

℮ Firstborn with firstborn: Both are too serious, too perfectionistic.

- Middle-born with middle-born: Neither is decisive enough.
- Last-born with last-born: Too much competition for attention.
- Only with only: You're both too needy.

3

Myers-Briggs– Inspired Typology

Remember in high school, when your guidance counselor would put you through endless multiple-choice tests to help you determine what careers you were best suited for? Psychologists rely on just such tests not only to help people identify their dream jobs but also to understand their personality and thus find more personal and professional fulfillment. One of the most popular and widely used of those tests is the Myers-Briggs type indicator (MBTI), which has been developed over the course of fifty years, often for career and personal counseling.

Rather than put you through the actual MBTI questionnaire, which is hundreds of pages long, we've distilled its principles into our own version here. The basic idea is the same: the test categorizes people into different types, based on a combination of personality traits. (In the test, you'll choose between four pairs of traits, which then leads you to identify your four-part "type.") No one type is better or worse than the others; differences between types simply reflect the differences between us and how we use our minds.

- How do you relate to others? Are you an extrovert, always the center of attention at parties, or an introvert, content to spend a quiet night at home?
- How much control do you like to have over your life? Are you a realist, who prefers routine and structure, or a visionary, who'd rather dream about the future with as much flexibility as possible?
- How do you take in information? Are you a feeler, who lets your heart guide you, or a thinker, who listens to your head instead?
- How do you make decisions? Are you an adapter, who enjoys spontaneity, or a decider, who'd rather have every detail planned in advance?

The following MBTI-inspired quiz will help you identify your personality type. Then we'll explain your unique strengths and gifts and how knowing your type can help you grow as a person.

What Type Are You?

There are four main categories in Myers-Briggs typology, and you'll be asked to choose between two personality options for each category. Answer the series of questions below, and keep track of your answers in each section. At the end, you'll be asked to combine your answers from each section to help you identify your type.

1. Are you an introvert or an extrovert?

Do you usually:
- (a) think things through before acting
- (b) act on impulse?

Do you:
- (a) work best on your own
- (b) thrive in interaction with other people?

Do you:
- (a) wait to be introduced
- (b) introduce yourself to others?

Do others think of you as:
- (a) too quiet and shy
- (b) too friendly and loud?

In social situations, do you:
- (a) prefer to be on the sidelines
- (b) talk easily and mingle with strangers?

If you answered mostly a's, you're an introvert (an I).
If you answered mostly b's, you're an extrovert (an E).

2. Are you a realist or a visionary?

Are you:
- (a) comfortable with routine
- (b) prefer to implement change?

Do you:
- (a) have a knack for details
- (b) have trouble remembering them?

Are you better at:
- (a) implementing ideas
- (b) coming up with them?

Do you prefer:
- (a) facts
- (b) dreams?

Do you prefer:
- (a) structure
- (b) flexibility?

Do you prefer to:
- (a) know what's coming
- (b) imagine the future?

If you answered mostly a's, you're a realist (an R).
If you answered mostly b's, you're a visionary (a V).

3. Are you a feeler or a thinker?

Do you believe
- (a) emotion rules over logic
- (b) logic rules over emotion?

Do you:
- (a) take criticism personally
- (b) present opinions with authority?

Do you:
- (a) like to hear a good story
- (b) prefer hard facts?

Do others see you as:
- (a) warm and companionable
- (b) cold and aloof?

Do you make decisions based on:
- (a) other people's feelings
- (b) logic and common sense?

If you answered mostly a's, you're a feeler (an F).
If you answered mostly b's, you're a thinker (a T).

4. Are you an adapter or a decider?

Are you:

    (a) often late to appointments

    (b) always punctual?

Do you:

    (a) enjoy spontaneity

    (b) prefer a planned life?

Do you value:

    (a) maintaining harmony

    (b) reaching goals?

Do you:

    (a) go with the flow

    (b) follow the preset route?

Do you:

    (a) procrastinate making decisions

    (b) make quick choices?

If you answered mostly a's, you're an adapter (an A).

If you answered mostly a's, you're a decider (a D).

Now take the four letters representing the traits you've identified for yourself and combine them, in order, to form a four-letter word. For example, if you are an introvert, realist, feeler, and adapter, then you're an IRFA. Then read on to learn more about your type.

ERFA

Nickname

The Entertainer

Defining Characteristics

Companionable, witty, charming, spontaneous, outgoing, superficial, trendy, and flighty

Challenges

To ERFAs, all the world's a stage, and you're always performing
on it—front and center. ERFAs live in the moment and love to
have a good time. Your natural exuberance makes you fun to be
with; others are drawn to your abundant warmth and optimism.
In turn, you feed on their attention; you couldn't stand to perform to an empty theater. You should try, though, to become
more stable and centered in your ceaseless pursuit of happiness.
You're easily bored, and can therefore be somewhat unreliable as
a partner or friend. Because of your high spirits, ERFAs are often lucky in attracting love, but you also need someone who is
more balancing and responsible than you in order to ground
you. At work, ERFAs are bursting with energy and ideas of ways
to do a better job. But you tend to have trouble meeting deadlines because you dislike structure and routine and anything that
limits the massive scope of your creative vision.

Famous ERFAs

Bill Clinton, Harvey Weinstein, Monica Lewinsky, Melanie
Griffith, John Travolta, Cher, Willard Scott, Goldie Hawn

ERFD

Nickname

The Caretaker

Defining Characteristics

Convivial, tenacious, warmhearted, talkative, popular, conscientious, cooperative, gushy, self-important, insecure, controlling, and overly sensitive

Challenges

ERFDs are the sensitive, nurturing caretakers of the world. The most sociable of all the types, you open yourself up to others because you want to help them solve their problems and ease their concerns. Harmony is your driving force; you dislike conflict and prefer to keep things pleasant at all times. You're very good at doing this, since you're always doing something nice for someone else—even at your own expense. You have a strong sense of responsibility and duty that often leads you to put the needs of others ahead of your own. You need to try, though, to make sure you're making yourself feel good while you're doing the same for everybody else. ERFDs have no trouble finding love, but you tend to have trouble staying in love—because your attentions can be so easily distracted by things and people outside your relationship. Try to remember to show as much affection and caring for your partner as you show to all the various causes that you work for. Your friends and loved ones would appreciate it if you'd become more dependable. At work, try to slow down the decision-making process and focus on one project at a time, since you tend to troubleshoot in all directions simultaneously. Because you're so concerned about solving all the problems of the world, the simpler ones—like balancing your checkbook or eating healthfully—don't get the attention they need.

Famous ERFDs

Oprah Winfrey, Jay Leno, Nicole Kidman, Cybill Shepherd, Ralph Nader

ERTA

Nickname

The Competitor

Defining Characteristics

Charismatic, heroic, dramatic, gregarious, fun loving, friendly, action oriented, reckless, self-centered, impatient, and blunt

Challenges

If there's a problem that needs solving, ERTAs are at the forefront, taking charge of the situation with dramatic flourish. ERTAs are brilliant negotiators, skilled at winning people over to their point of view. As an ERTA, you prefer to live in the here and now, focusing on immediate results. You tend to move and talk fast to get things done and move on to the next step. You dislike long explanations that eat up your time and attention. You're too impatient for that—you're a risk taker who lives a fast-paced lifestyle, and you wouldn't have it any other way. Given their high energy, ERTAs are usually great athletes who keep themselves in enviable shape. You need to learn, though, to follow through with promises and commitments made—in all areas of your life. You like the thrill of the chase—and the comfort of intimacy doesn't offer that to you. As an ERTA, you get caught up in the passion at the start of a romance, but when it starts to wane, you tend to lose interest. In business, too, you tend to job-op, leaving each position as soon as you've mastered it. You're better off working for yourself: ERTAs are natural entrepreneurs who can thrive in their own businesses. It's very important that you're allowed the flexibility to come and go as you please, since you don't like routine and prefer to work on your own. But sometimes collaboration can bring great successes; you should remind yourself that others might have ideas worth exploring.

Famous ERTAs

Michael Jordan, Elton John, Bob Hope, Sean Connery, Sarah Ferguson, Wynonna Judd

ERTD

Nickname

The Supervisor

Defining Characteristics

Orderly, industrious, logical, practical, traditional, hardworking, uptight, indifferent, calculating, overpowering, and rigid

Challenges

ERTDs want to make the world a better place—and they know just how to do it. You've got exacting ideas for how to fix what's broken and bring order to chaotic situations, and can skillfully rally people around you to get things done. You like to be in charge, directing all those around you, but you're often disappointed when your perfectionist standards aren't met. You need to learn tolerance and to balance work with play. ERTDs tend to bring the same practical attitude toward love as they have toward life in general. You're attracted to those who can offer you status or beauty, those who won't challenge your authority. Don't be so quick to sneer at emotional honesty as you usually do, tossing it off as a sign of weakness. Try to learn to value feelings as much as facts and to encourage others to share their ideas with you. With your take-charge attitude, ERTDs have a natural head for business. You're an ideal executive, able to lead any group or company and run it efficiently. But you need to learn to focus as much on the needs of your employees as on the needs of your business.

Famous ERTDs

Donald Trump, Martha Stewart, Alec Baldwin, Michael Eisner, Michael Dukakis, Colin Powell, Shirley Temple, Dana Delaney

EVFA

Nickname

The Explorer

Defining Characteristics

Bubbly, persuasive, self-starter, enthusiastic, high-spirited, ingenious, imaginative, flexible, idealistic, scattered, grandiose, and insensitive

Challenges

EVFAs have a restless hunger that drives them constantly to seek out new ideas and experiences; as an EVFA, you live life as if each day were the ultimate adventure. To you, life is an exciting drama, and you want to spend it doing anything and everything that catches your fancy. But in your ceaseless search for the next big thing, you tend to ignore the details of daily life. You rely heavily on your ability to improvise instead of preparing in advance, which usually serves you well but can leave others around you feeling ignored or slighted. You must try to become less restless. EVFAs are always lured by the sexy stranger in the corner who catches their eye. You've had a string of passionate, intense relationships that have died out as your attention wandered elsewhere. Try to be more meditative and constant in each relationship and to show more empathy and commitment. If you want to find lasting love, you'll need to demonstrate to your partner that you've got the endurance and the patience to be trusted at all times—even the dull moments. Like most extroverts, EVFAs hate the structure and routine of traditional workplaces. As a result, you may go through several different careers, trying on new roles as each piques your interest. Luckily, your gregarious nature means you have little trouble adapting, whether you find yourself in sales or journalism or teaching. You'll stay in any job as long as you find it challenging.

Famous EVFAs

Madonna, Matt Lauer, Emma Thompson, Robin Williams, Madeleine Albright, Dustin Hoffman, Sissy Spacek, Nick Nolte, Tom Hanks, Brad Pitt, Tina Turner

EVFD

Nickname

The Mentor

Defining Characteristics

Compelling, decisive, magnanimous, responsive, social, popular, sympathetic, sensitive, bossy, illusionary, manipulative, controlling, and didactic

Challenges

EVFDs believe in the potential of others and want to help them realize all that they can be. As an EVFD, you're an outstanding leader because you feel true concern for what others think and want. But you can also be somewhat aggressive and heavy-handed in your efforts to help others achieve. Try to be more thoughtful and less insistent on having your own way at the expense of others, especially in matters of the heart. EVFDs are sensitive, sharing lovers, but you can be overly forceful in getting your own way and dictating the terms of the relationship. Try to become more flexible and allow your partner to have a voice in guiding the path of your relationship. EVFDs are effective managers because you can convince everyone that your way is the right way. You thrive in careers like counseling or teaching, where you can lead and inspire others. But be sure to take time to check your motivations and morals; make sure you're keeping others' needs in mind as you lead them toward your pursuit of your greater vision.

Famous EVFDs

Deepak Chopra, Elizabeth Dole, Barbara Walters, Ronald Reagan, Jane Fonda, Lee Iacocca, Oliver Stone

EVTA

Nickname

The Inventor

Defining Characteristics

Outspoken, entrepreneurial, inspired, courageous, creative, quick, ingenious, multitalented, alert, resourceful, impulsive, narcissistic, abstract, and assertive

Challenges

EVTAs love the creative process and the challenge of coming up with innovative solutions to intricate puzzles. You're often so enthusiastic about new ideas and the possibility of change that it's hard to keep you grounded. EVTAs rarely sit still; you move on impulse, and you readily indulge your every whim, from food (you need to watch what you eat) to fashion (your closet could use a bit of cleaning out). In doing so, though, you often trample on the feelings of those closest to you, albeit unintentionally. You should try to become more aware of your own personal accountability, and more sensitive to others. You enjoy the support and nurturing that relationships can provide, but your restlessness can be unsettling to a partner. You're always surprised when your relationships become problematic, as they often tend to do. Others can be put off by your love of debating; your tendency to argue over even the most minor points can come off as argumentative and abrasive, especially at work. Schedules and routines terrify you; as an EVTA, you need independence and flexibility in order to fully maximize your inventive genius and create your miracles. But your impulsiveness means you often walk away before a project is completed. You need to be more willing to see projects through to completion, and more receptive to others' suggestions.

Famous EVTAs

Julia Roberts, Gwyneth Paltrow, Jennifer Aniston, Johnny Depp, Daniel Day-Lewis, Whoopi Goldberg, Billy Joel, David Letterman, Sharon Stone, Ted Turner

EVTD

Nickname

The Strategist

Defining Characteristics

Decisive, protective, strong, forceful, dynamic, assertive, outspoken, intelligent, harsh, dictatorial, and inflexible

Challenges

EVTDs are the leaders of any army or team, the ultimate field marshals. As an EVTD, your basic driving force is your need to be a leader. In any situation—personal or professional—you tend to seek out a position of responsibility and never relinquish it once you get there. But you also tend to get somewhat dictatorial. In the pursuit of the courage of your convictions, you often run roughshod over anyone who stands in your path, even innocent bystanders. Try to become more feeling and flexible as you lead, and to remember to listen to the other voices around you. As an EVTD, you've got plenty of admirers because of your strength and determination. You tend to seek out partners who are pliable, who'll bend to your whims. Encourage your mates and friends to instead stand up to you and challenge you. Not surprisingly, EVTDs are often the generals and presidents of companies, driven by their determined, authoritative nature. You're most likely to be successful in the business world, which suits your forceful style of management. Because you have no natural patience for mistakes or inefficiency, you should make a concerted effort to become more sympathetic and responsive to your staff. That's the best way to win their loyalty.

Famous EVTDs

Colin Powell, Michael Ovitz, Bill Gates, Barbara Bush, George Steinbrenner

IRFA

Nickname

The Free Spirit

Defining Characteristics

Affable, passionate, sensitive, kind, modest, faithful, flexible, open-minded, self-critical, depressive, and reserved

Challenges

IRFAs dance to the beat of a different drummer—in fact, they're often the first to recognize that drummer's talents. As an IRFA, you're an artist who lives to create works of beauty, from a gorgeous painting to a family you can be proud of. You prefer to sit back and enjoy the moment, and you don't want it spoiled by haste or exertion. You know that things will get done eventually, so you're generally relaxed about timing. You'd rather spend your time having a deep, intimate conversation than breaking a sweat mowing the lawn. You're not interested in leading or in stirring up conflict; you don't want to force your opinions on others. You're so focused, in fact, on the needs of others that you tend to neglect yourself—often to the detriment of your own health and well-being. Try to become more self-revealing in public and in private; you're far too likely to keep your desires buried deep inside. Try to be more openly demonstrative in relationships and more forthright about your feelings. And try to be less critical of yourself, which can turn off prospective partners. That also holds true for your work life: IRFAs want work to be more than just a job. To you, it's not about earning money, it's about helping others, especially as a teacher, counselor, or minister. Just be sure that you're getting the attention you need, too. Are you getting paid what you should? Are you getting the recognition and promotions you deserve?

Famous IRFAs

Rita Wilson, Lauryn Hill, Kelly Preston, Kate Capshaw, Katherine Graham, Queen Elizabeth

IRFD

Nickname

The Protector

Defining Characteristics

Conscientious, giving, dependable, thorough, considerate, perceptive, stable, warm and kindhearted, dependent, unassertive, and doubtful

Challenges

IRFDs are deeply concerned with how other people feel, and intensely loyal to their nearest and dearest. You'll volunteer unselfishly to make sure all their needs are met, and can be depended upon to follow through—at all hours and to any personal expense. You have a very hard time saying no. But if you want to take better care of others, you need to take better care of yourself first. Try to become more self-caring and understand that your own needs are as important as those of others. You're attracted to partners who are powerful and who command respect, which you're only too happy to give them. But you should try to be more assertive, to identify, value, and express your own needs; otherwise, you may easily be taken for granted by a more dominant mate or friend.

Famous IRFDs

Tipper Gore, Betty Ford, Debbie Reynolds, George W. Bush

Nickname

The Analyzer

Defining Characteristics

Cool, confident, realistic, practical, curious, stimulating, fearless, observant, stodgy, stiff, rash, cold, dispassionate, judgmental, and impulsive

Challenges

IRTAs enjoy observing how things work, taking them apart and putting them back together again, so they can understand what makes them function the way they do. You love the challenge of solving problems and making discoveries on your own. But IRTAs aren't exactly the world's greatest romantics. You're far too intense and analytical to let yourself be swept off your feet. You think more with your head than with your heart, and you expect your companions to do the same. It wouldn't hurt, though, to try to become warmer and more open. Try to show more affection and thoughtfulness to your partner instead of bringing your cold, analytic approach to every relationship. With your indefatigable focus and perseverance, you're well suited for any job that requires extraordinary precision, like surgeon, sculptor, engineer, or accountant. Your love of problem solving serves you well at work—but you can't sit alone behind a desk all day. Try to interact more with your colleagues and engage them in an exchange of ideas. They may be even be able to (gasp!) help you solve that puzzle you've been trying to tackle.

Famous IRTAs

Hillary Rodham Clinton, Robert Redford, Clint Eastwood

IRTD

Nickname

The Planner

Defining Characteristics

Dependable, practical, orderly, logical, realistic, thorough, responsible, well organized, hardworking, somber, worrisome, depressive, and humorless

Challenges

As an IRTD, you accomplish any task you set your mind to by thoroughly drawing up detailed plans in advance and planning for any possible eventuality. You enjoy taking on huge amounts of responsibility, and once you do, everything else goes on the back burner. You'd never walk away from a project or leave it incomplete. You want to achieve recognition through achievement, but since you tend to take on so much, you rarely let yourself relax and let yourself enjoy a good time. IRTDs aren't the type to fall passionately in love; you're uncomfortable expressing affection and emotion. But you'd enjoy a strong, committed partnership with someone who shares your commitment. Try to show more grace and humor, to look more for the beauty marks instead of the scars. IRTDs prefer to work alone—and you often work long hours, investing all your energy in your labor. You thrive in highly demanding positions, which carry great expectations of your performance, like foreman, judge, or doctor. But such high, unrelenting stress levels can wreak havoc with your health.

Famous *IRTDs*

Janet Reno, Al Gore, Anita Hill, Katharine Hepburn, Winona Ryder, Bill Bradley

IVFA

Nickname

The Harmonizer

Defining Characteristics

Romantic, mystical, earnest, thoughtful, reflective, idealistic, self-effacing, withholding, and martyrlike

Challenges

With your ever-present pair of rose-colored glasses, IVFAs just want to make the world a better place. You disdain conflict, preferring instead to simply go with the flow. You're spiritual, graceful, and emotionally devoted to all those in your life. You care little about your own possessions, and derive your sense of honor and purpose from giving to others. Along the way, you tend to bite off more than you can chew, but somehow you manage to get it all done in the end—often, though, at a price to yourself that you can't always pay. But you have such impossibly high ideals that you often set yourself up for disappointment when things inevitably don't live up to your expectations, especially in matters of the heart. IVFAs are the saints and angels of the working world. Your innate tendency to be caring and selfless manifests itself in the work that you choose—counseling, psychiatry, social services. You need to be sure, though, not to let your work overtake you. Remember to ask for support when you need it.

Famous IVFAs

Rosie O'Donnell, Julia Roberts, Paul Simon, Mario Cuomo, Michelle Pfeiffer, Robert De Niro

IVFD

Nickname

The Individualist

Defining Characteristics

Imaginative, creative, decisive, sensitive, persevering, original, quietly forceful, conscientious, concerned for others, sloppy, unrealistic, restless, and stubborn

Challenges

The rarest of all personality types in the Myers-Briggs system, IVFDs are complex, highly individualistic people. As an IVFD, you want to live with a sense of purpose; you're motivated and fulfilled by helping others. But you want to do so practically and realistically. You're respected by others for sticking to your firm principles and your clear conviction on how to serve the common good. You're willing to do what is needed to help others, and to put everything you have into any project, but you're also grounded enough to realize that living an idealistic life can lead to a great deal of stress. You need to learn to be at peace with yourself and to recognize the limits of even your admirable powers. In relationships, you're too analytical to let yourself get swept up in a wave of passion; you're more likely to let love come to you. You seek out those who are also reserved but who can also inspire you to open your heart. Let yourself express your feelings physically, with frequent hugs and pats on the back.

Famous IVFDs

Warren Beatty, Demi Moore, Richard Gere, Jimmy Carter

IVTA

Nickname

The Discoverer

Defining Characteristics

Individualistic, independent, meticulous, smart, quiet, reserved, constricted, humorless, detached, restless, and temperamental

Challenges

Known for their active, restless imagination, IVTAs are thinkers, theorizers, and analyzers. Faced with any situation, you wonder how it can be improved upon. You see new patterns and connections where others simply see what's always been done. It's hard to get to know you well, though, because you've built a shield around you that's nearly impenetrable. The absentminded professor in you forgets to eat, forgets to exercise as you spend hours on end struggling to solve whatever puzzle is before you. Though you enjoy the complex challenges you create for yourself, you need to let yourself enjoy life just a bit more, to become more lighthearted, spontaneous, and uninhibited. IVTAs shudder at the idea of romance; it's just so impractical and illogical. You need to let yourself give in to love, to become more simple, childlike, and wondrous at the emotional power of romance. You have few close friends; you don't easily open up to others and share your feelings and thoughts with them. Try, though, to be more direct and expressive with those you're close to; let them see that you are capable of warmth and emotional honesty.

Famous IVTAs

Albert Einstein, Meryl Streep, Helen Hunt, Neil Simon, Steve Martin, Meg Ryan, Andrew Lloyd Webber, Garry Trudeau, Woody Allen, Gary Larsen, Sigourney Weaver

IVTD

Nickname

The Director

Defining Characteristics

Independent, efficient, critical, independent, determined, analytical, withdrawn, somber, aloof, stubborn, and reserved

Challenges

IVTDs are conceptualizers who have a vision of how they can improve the ways in which they live and work, and pursue that vision with all the manifold skills in their arsenal. As an IVTD, you're a natural leader with an original mind, great drive, and the power to organize a job and carry it through, with or without the help of others. You're self-confident and pragmatic, you see the reason behind things, and decisions come easily to you. You value knowledge and competence, and disdain failure that doesn't meet your high standards. In fact, your "I'm king of the world" attitude can be rather off-putting. Dispassionate and distanced, IVTDs bring a sober, intellectual approach to love. As an IVTD, you tend not to be demonstrative, which others can misinterpret as lack of caring. IVTDs tend to have problems unwinding and letting go of the problems that race around their minds. You should try to become more open and playful, and learn to enjoy the fruits of your efforts.

Famous IVTDs

James Cameron, Harrison Ford, Barbra Streisand, John Malkovich, Marilyn Quayle

The Enneagram

Are you a perfectionist, who must have everything done just the right way? Or are you an adventurer, who seeks excitement and thrills in every moment of every day? According to the enneagram, there are nine types of people, each with a unique way of seeing the world and interacting with it. By learning your own "type"—as well as the types of those around you, at home and at work—you can increase your fulfillment in your life and in your relationships with others.

The enneagram is a nine-pointed star within a circle, with each point representing one of the nine personality types. (See diagram, page 83) Though the enneagram gained mainstream attention in the 1960s, its roots have been traced to everything from Middle Eastern philosophy to Pythagorean theory. The word itself comes from Greek, with *ennea* meaning "nine" and *grammos* meaning "diagram."

Each personality type is characterized by a specific guiding "passion" around which the personality has taken shape. This passion then influences how we think, feel, and behave around

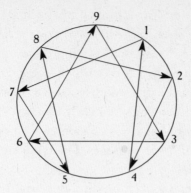

others. No one type is better or healthier than another; it's simply a matter of our different perceptions. We all strive for different goals and use different means of achieving them. You should therefore use the enneagram not as a tool for judging others but for stimulating awareness and understanding of them and of yourself. By recognizing a person's enneagram type, you'll be clued in to insider information on his or her deepest motivations.

Enneagram theory holds that in childhood, each of us, based on our innate talents and abilities, developed a specific psychological strategy (or defense mechanism) as a way of getting attention and avoiding physical and emotional discomfort. That strategy then shaped our personalities and helped determine our enneagram type. Though this defense mechanism can sometimes hinder our relationships and prevent us from being as effective and happy as we can be, it can also be transformed into something productive. We can all learn to turn our negative tendencies into healthier responses.

Your type follows you through life, but it can be modified by your life experiences. Each point in the enneagram is connected to two others by internal arrows. When you're relaxed, you take on the positive qualities of the number your arrow points to; when you're stressed, you take on the negative qualities of the number of the arrow that points to your type. For example, when Ones are relaxed, they may become more playful, like a Seven; when they're stressed, they may act more self-absorbed and withdrawn, like a Four. You likely also have "wings," or lean more to one side of the circle or another—Ones, say, may tend toward aspects of Twos or Nines. The types are, after all, connected by the circle.

When it comes to relationships, there aren't necessarily better or worse pairings of enneagram types—likes tend to attract likes, just as opposites tend to attract too. But certain pairings can better bring out the best in each other, compensating for each other's weaknesses while fostering personal growth.

So how can you find out what type you are? Psychologists use complicated, pages-long questionnaires, but we've tried to simplify matters. After each type, we've listed five statements. If you identify or agree with at least four of those statements, chances are that's your type. Some of you may see yourself in more than one type; after all, we're multifaceted people, not easily pigeonholed. Look for the number that most strongly identifies your patterns of behavior. Another clue is your reaction to the description of the type you've identified as yours: The number you'd least like to be is probably the one that you are. (Sorry!)

One

THE PERFECTIONIST

1. I'm hardworking and organized.
2. I don't like it when people break rules or are late.
3. I'm rarely spontaneous; I plan as much as I can in advance.

4. I don't have enough time to relax.

5. I believe in making the world a better place.

Ones are swimming with good intentions: you want to improve yourself and others. You're known and valued for your integrity and high principles; you see things as right or wrong and are bothered when things aren't "fair." That often means that you set impossibly high standards, then are constantly struggling to meet them. You're highly critical of yourself and others when those standards aren't met, and may procrastinate endlessly for fear of making a mistake. You're oversensitive about your weaknesses, and tend to have trouble relaxing and being playful. You probably learned this behavior from overly critical parents, who valued and rewarded achievement over all else.

Strengths

Conscientious, self-disciplined, idealistic, ethical, well organized, good problem solvers, and bring out the best in others

Weaknesses

Critical, self-righteous, judgmental, dogmatic, rigid, petty, and tense

Overall Self-improvement Goals

To turn your tendency to criticize into acceptance by learning to relax, to trust your capabilities, and to enjoy your accomplishments. You should take regular vacations, watch a funny, silly movie every now and then (just because), and reward yourself regularly with special treats. And remember not to be so hard on people. Forgive them for their mistakes—and don't forget to forgive yourself, too.

Romance

You need to learn to see your partner's unique characteristics as beautiful facets in a diamond, rather than fatal flaws. Remember always to look for ways to express your gratitude and appreciation—not just constructive criticism. Because you have difficulty trusting that anyone can live up to your exacting standards, you need a partner who is reliable and dependable, someone who won't let you down. A One's partner should be easygoing and have an appreciation for life—not someone who is exacting, stern, or power hungry, which will further fuel your own anxiety and sometimes obsessive drive. Since you need to be reassured constantly about your own worth, your ideal partner should be a nurturer who will commend you often, appreciating your strengths as well as your weaknesses, and—here's the big one—loving you all the same.

Friendship

As friends, Ones need to work on being more forgiving and accepting. Be careful to show patience and understanding with those you care about, especially during tough times, when life isn't going as it should or a friend isn't acting as you would expect or hope. Ideal friends for Ones have a great sense of humor, and don't take life too seriously. They can appreciate your accomplishments, but they don't value you because of them. And they don't take criticism too seriously: if you snapped at them, they'd laugh it off. They can handle the anger and the brittleness a One often expresses, because they see your warm heart underneath.

Health and Fitness

One word: moderation. You can get obsessed with a type of workout or diet plan, so you must exercise moderation in your fitness routine and diet. It's easy for Ones to stray into being un-erringly strict or bingeing out of control, especially if you've been depriving yourself on a diet, so be sure to set up a middle-of-the-road exercise and diet plan that acknowledges the neces-sary requirements for good health but also provides built-in enjoyment rewards.

Work

Because of their efficiency and organization, Ones tend to shine at their work, especially while holding positions of authority or responsibility. You excel in jobs where procedures need to be fol-lowed (teachers, accountants), where organization and meticu-lous detail are key (scientists), and where you can be the arbiters of correct behavior (police officers, judges). You're also great at meeting deadlines—though you do have to watch out for pro-crastination—and you can be good team players, as long as you respect your team's goals and ethics. You should strive to help others achieve your high standards, but be forgiving when they don't; it's important for you to maintain a good sense of humor with those whose work isn't as impeccable as yours. Your ideal job should have a substantive moral agenda (like a philanthropic cause you believe in), something that improves the quality of life for others, because you are so driven by your ethics and your sense of right and wrong.

Money

At any given moment, Ones can report to the penny how much money is in her 401(k) plan. Your bank accounts are never over-drawn, and you never bounce checks, because you worry end-lessly about not having enough money. While there's nothing wrong with financial prudence, you should try to use your con-cerns in a positive way, to make sure you have funds for vacation as well as for retirement, for example. Set aside a small sum each month as play money, and let yourself splurge every once in a while, even if just on a new book you've been eyeing. Be careful, though. Ones can be creatures of extremes, and you may get so wound up after months of rigidity and miserliness that you blow all your savings in a mad shopping spree.

How to Recognize a One

You're dressed impeccably from head to toe, without a stain or a frayed thread anywhere. Your clothing is classic, tailored, and elegant. You wouldn't be caught dead in hippie chic or ultratrendy clothes. Ones set the standards in conservative fashion.

Famous Ones

Hillary Rodham Clinton, Miss Manners, Ralph Nader, Margaret Thatcher, Pope John Paul II, Nurse Ratched (from *One Flew over the Cuckoo's Nest*)

Two

THE GIVER

1. I like it when people come to me for help—I need to feel needed.
2. I have trouble asking for what I want.
3. I'm more comfortable giving than receiving.
4. I have a hard time saying no to others.
5. I'm often lonely, and I hate being lonely more than anything else.

Twos are the best friends anyone could want: because of your need to be loved and appreciated, you're tremendously caring of others. You excel at making people feel special. As children, Twos were rewarded for pleasing, and they tended to support their parents emotionally. You want to be indispensable in the lives of those around you, but it often comes at a price—you expect repayment in the form of affection and approval. You also tend to become *too* involved, to overextend yourself to too many good causes. You end up feeling physically and emotionally burned out, and unvalued, because you haven't been acknowledging your own needs. You martyr yourself, then resent others for putting you in that position of vulnerability.

Strengths

Compassionate, sensitive, generous, nurturing, empathetic, and concerned

Weaknesses

Dependent, needy, possessive, intrusive, and manipulative

Overall Self-improvement Goals

To value yourself more, to see receiving as important as giving. When you do give to others, you should do so unconditionally and with humility. Do things for yourself that don't involve others—and don't be afraid to set limits or be assertive with other people.

Romance

Be honest about your needs at the very start of a relationship, and allow your partner to offer you the same emotional and physical help that you so readily give. Because you tend to give in order to feel loved, you need someone who is constant so you can never question his or her love. You need to be reassured often of your own worth and attractiveness, so your ideal partner should also be generous and free with compliments so you will never feel the need to question his or her loyalty.

Friendship

Surround yourself with people who can see through your giving exterior and remind you that you have your own needs that must be tended. It's easy to take advantage of Twos, so you need friends who will say, "Okay, enough about me. What about you?" as often as necessary. You must remember to include yourself in any relationship equation as one who matters.

Health and Fitness

Because you're so busy taking care of others, you tend to neglect your own body, either by eating too much or not getting enough exercise. You may forget that your own body and fitness regimen needs the same kind of caring that you lavish on others. You need to be reminded to treat your body the way you would treat the bodies of the people you love.

Work

Twos are people people. You excel in any kind of job requiring friendliness, warmth, and security; you exude a sense of well-being in any kind of work situation. You make the best nurses and counselors, and the best people to support leaders. You work hard, but you don't make your own need for recognition clear enough. Be sure that you get the rewards and accolades you deserve.

Money

Need a loan? Call on a Two—you thrive on rescuing others from any kind of problem, including financial difficulties. But you need to remember to focus on your own financial welfare, too. Your pocketbook and portfolio should be as well tended as those of your partner or best friend. Remember to seek financial advice, not just give.

How to Recognize a Two

You're the person clad in soft, inviting fabrics—others always want to touch and hug you.

Famous Twos

Melanie Griffith, Sally Field, Monica Lewinsky, Glenn Close in *Fatal Attraction*, John Ritter, Alan Alda, Bill Cosby, Mr. Rogers

Three

THE ACHIEVER

1. I'm successful, optimistic, and always busy.
2. I don't let anything stand in the way of my ultimate goals.
3. I get frustrated with incompetence and inadequacy.
4. I don't like it when people say no to me.
5. I'll be happy after the next promotion.

The Three's mantel is cluttered with prizes and awards; you're an unrivaled winner and champion in whatever activity you pursue. Productive and success oriented, you are an enthusiastic, effective leader. As a child, you were prized for your achievements; your performance was rewarded rather than your feelings or emotional connections in other people's lives. As a result you're so afraid of failure and rejection that you can never relax; you're obsessed with your image and with appearances. Your sense of your own value comes not from how you view yourself but the prestige and accolades others heap on you. Success is more important to you than anything else; you'll sacrifice yourself to your career, and expect the same of others. Because you're so uncomfortable with your own feelings, you have difficulty forming intimate relationships and can lose friends in the frenzy of competition.

Strengths

Upbeat, confident, successful, steady, self-assured, ambitious, and competitive

Weaknesses

Narcissistic, defensive, shallow, impatient, image conscious, hostile, type A, and workaholic

Overall Self-improvement Goals

To transform your image consciousness and workaholism into inner conviction by learning to accept your own competence without external validation. You should allow yourself time to relax and do the things you love—outside of work.

Romance

Be more willing to spend a quiet night at home—the kind of quality time necessary just to get to know another person without necessarily moving the relationship forward. You are at your best when you're in relationships with people who value your unceasing drive as part of your essential magnetism.

Friendship

Being a friend to a Three requires energy. Ideal friends for you are people who are active, eager for fun and adventure, competitive in a healthy way—people who can relax and talk openly and honestly about their fears, which you are terrified of doing yourself. Remember to be sure to support your friends in their goals and make time to listen to them about their concerns.

Health and Fitness

As natural enthusiasts, Threes have no problem staying in shape. You need to make sure, however, that your inner self is as well toned as your outer self. You can get so caught up in your external image—Threes are the people who line plastic surgeons' offices and who experiment with steroids and diet drugs—you need to remember that the outside only looks as good as outside, that what matters is the quality of what's inside, not just the surface.

Work

Threes are the golden boys and girls of the company—you set the standards for the rest of the pack. Ideal careers for Threes are in business, politics, and sales. You're also natural leaders who can make others feel good just because they're part of your team. You should take time, though, to get to know your co-workers as well as you know your own accomplishments. And you should make sure that you take enough vacation and the occasional day off—otherwise, you'll work around the clock, 365 days a year. Because of your overwhelming need for recognition, you tend to be unduly concerned with impressing superiors.

Money

Threes are often amply rewarded financially for their many accomplishments. While you therefore usually have a generous paycheck, you do need to keep an eye on your budget. Caught up in the relentless pursuit of image, you could overextend yourself financially in an effort to impress others.

How to Recognize a Three

Though you won't take fashion risks, you are the trendsetters, from a classic point of view. You wouldn't wear a body-hugging, navel-baring outfit, but you would be the first to wear alligator shoes, to sport the hot new look that everyone's talking about.

Famous Threes

Tom Cruise, O. J. Simpson, Oprah Winfrey, Elizabeth Dole, Madonna

Four

THE ROMANTIC

1. I'm waiting for the love of my life to come along.
2. I'll do anything to avoid the ordinary, the mundane.
3. I'm often told that I'm too sensitive; I can cry at the drop of a hat.
4. Sometimes I feel that no one really understands me.
5. I appreciate creativity and the arts—literature, film, theater, museums.

Fours are the artists, the creators, the Renaissance men and women. Sensitive and passionate, you're endlessly searching for the meaning of life and you strive to avoid experiencing boredom or being ordinary in any way. You want to understand other people's deepest feelings, and be understood in the same way. (Of all the nine types, you're the most in touch with your inner feelings.) But you can turn cold and peevish if you're misunderstood or hurt. Your childhood may have been solitary and unhappy; feeling abandoned by one or both parents, you turned inward for self-satisfaction. You tend to be attracted to the unavailable, the missing, the flawed. Intimidated by social interaction, you've turned to artistic fields as a means of communication.

Strengths

Creative, emotional, risk taking, intuitive, expressive, and passionate

Weaknesses

Soap-opera-ish, withdrawn, self-absorbed, and melancholic

Overall Self-improvement Goals

To let go of some of your self-absorption and turn it into equanimity. Learn to see life as an interplay of loss and love *without* regret.

Romance

You give yourself over to every endeavor completely, especially love affairs. You're prone to becoming involved in intense, tormented, doomed relationships. You need a romantic partner who is stable and reliable, who loves your drama and the colorfulness of who are you are—but who won't go on the roller coaster with you. Make an effort to focus more on the joys of steadiness, and aim to be more emotionally dependable.

Friendship

You tend to be self-involved, which can be off-putting to your friends. Try to work at being more other-directed by practicing the art of responsive listening. You should seek out friends who love to listen to you, who will support you through all your ups and downs. But your friends should also let you know that there are limits and boundaries in relationships. They should be honest with you when you go to extremes.

Health and Fitness

You love to be fit (from an artistic point of view, beautiful bodies do look better), but you prefer to exercise in only the most beautiful of settings—say, jog through a wooded park while listening to Mozart on a Walkman. There's nothing wrong with that, as long as you remember to do it on a regular basis. As for diet, you tend to take the gourmet route—you love to sample all of life's indulgences. While you shouldn't get stuck in calorie counting, you do need to learn to enjoy the best in small doses.

Work

Not surprisingly, Fours are unrivaled poets, musicians, actors, and artists. But you can also function well in traditional office settings, as the visionaries of the company. Just remember, as a Four it's important that you value punctuality and predictability as well as original genius. When working with Fours, be sure to separate any job criticism from personal criticism, because Fours are very sensitive and tend to take everything personally.

Money

Fours tend to feel that money is too mundane a concept to be worthy of their attention. Your finances are likely in complete disarray; your retirement accounts—if you even have any—contain the bare minimum. You need to think of money as something that will give you more artistic freedom—that will be motivation for you to cultivate money.

How to Recognize a Four

It'll come as no shock that you are the people who define the edges of style. You're the signatures of originality. Think Gianni Versace, Dolce & Gabbana. Fours thrive on wearing clothes that shock and delight, but you wouldn't be caught dead in Nikes or a three-piece suit (unless you were wearing them in a completely untraditional way).

Famous Fours

Elizabeth Taylor, Romeo and Juliet, Madame Bovary, Greta Garbo, Kate Winslet as Marianne in *Sense and Sensibility*, Jennifer Lopez, Sarah Jessica Parker, Kelly Preston

Five

THE OBSERVER

1. I want to know and understand everything that's going on around me.
2. I'm uncomfortable around big groups of people.
3. I need time to myself.
4. People often ask me what I'm thinking.
5. I get irritated when I have to repeat things or explain myself.

Fives can always be found on the sidelines, away from the action—but that's where they love to be. You prefer to know everything that's going on around you rather than being part of the action. You're a thinker, not a doer. The most intellectually gifted of all the types, you are also highly independent. As a child, you may have felt intruded upon, that your privacy was stolen. Whenever you could, you'd stay in your room behind closed doors; otherwise, you'd erect emotional barriers. As an adult, you not only keep physical distance from others but also emotional distance. You tend to feel drained by commitment and other people's needs. You keep your feelings to yourself, and protect your privacy religiously. You simply don't want to waste time or energy on the drama of other people's lives.

Strengths

Profoundly insightful, analytic, perceptive, cerebral, and self-sufficient

Weaknesses

Paranoid, cynical, self-pitying, emotionally remote, arrogant, and detached

Overall Self-improvement Goals

To get involved; to turn your detachment into compassion. Your pursuit of knowledge needn't be from a distance.

Romance

Fives approach romance intellectually. You should try, however, to be more expressive and engaged in your relationships. Work on being more willing to share more of yourself without waiting for your partner to reveal all. Your ideal partner values you for your intelligence, not your attractiveness, and creates a safe environment for you to reveal your carefully guarded thoughts, ideas, and fears.

Friendship

Fives don't easily warm up to others, but you can work on this by sharing more details about your rich inner life. This will demonstrate to friends your feelings of trust and confidence in them. Seek out open-minded, adventurous people who can help you open up your heart to untested experiences.

Health and Fitness

For Fives, your minds—not your bodies—are your first priority. So you need to make every effort to balance your preoccupation with thinking with a regimen of body-centered diet and exercise. Don't use treadmills or stair climbers, or any machine that allows you to zone out while exercising; instead, focus on activities like yoga and dance that require your mental presence. As for diet, Fives tend to be finicky eaters, so make sure that you have varied and interesting food choices—and that you remember to eat at all!

Work

Given your intellectual prowess, Fives are the breakthrough minds of any organization. You're the inventors, the engineers, the theorists, so you should work in professions that take advantage of your original ideas, your ability to research, and your thorough method of interpretation. Fives aren't the strongest supervisors, since they tend to operate from behind closed doors and are best at working alone. When you do work with others, you should make an effort to be clear and expressive about your ideas and impressions.

Money

Howard Hughes is a classic example of a Five at his worst: someone so carried away with fear and withholding that he doesn't allow himself or anyone close to him the joy of spending. As a Five, you need to be wary of pinching your wallet to extremes. You're a champion of voluntary simplicity, but you shouldn't turn it into involuntary poverty.

How to Recognize a Five

Fives can be spotted a mile away, thanks to their utter lack of fashion sense and mismatched clothes. You're not particularly concerned with style at all; in fact, most of the time, you don't even know what you've put on. Left unmonitored, you can come up with rather original combinations, like plaids with paisley.

Famous Fives

Al Gore, Albert Einstein, Bill Gates, Johnny Carson, Ebenezer Scrooge, Sigmund Freud

Six

THE QUESTIONER

1. I often feel insecure and plagued by doubt.
2. I prefer to have someone else set rules and boundaries.
3. I identify with the underdog in most situations.
4. I'm loyal and devoted to my friends and family.
5. I tend to procrastinate.

The ultimate team player, Sixes love being told what to do. You're committed and loyal to others; in return, you want to feel secure and taken care of. You encourage the establishment of boundaries, rules, and authority figures and tend to seek security in your loyalty to someone else or something outside yourself. You're not comfortable acting independently. When you were a child, your parents were erratic and unpredictable, so you learned to hesitate, to look for danger signs before taking action. As an adult, you therefore often procrastinate. Thinking, for you, often replaces doing.

Strengths

Loyal, courageous, devoted, committed, responsible, and dutiful

Weaknesses

Dependent, childishly rebellious, fanatical, fearful, negative, defensive, and paranoid

Overall Self-improvement Goals

To turn fear and doubt into courage and self-possession by learning ways to find security internally. You need to become self-approving and to enter into a healthy, not dependent, relationship with authority.

Romance

Be more vulnerable in sharing your dreams and visions, letting your partner knows what drives you and what you deeply desire. You should be with someone who unconditionally approves of who you are. Your ideal partner should praise you for your inner convictions without endorsing your fears.

Friendship

Because Sixes tend to be so insecure, you need to be more inclusive with your friends, opening up to others and letting them know what you need from them in order to feel safe. You're best off with an equal, someone who is not easily caught up in power plays but who enjoys sharing and twinship—"we're in this together." Because Sixes have difficulty trusting, it's important for you to enter into friendship with people whom you can disagree with or challenge without fear of damage to the relationship.

Health and Fitness

Because of your commitment to the team, Sixes can be wonderful athletes. But you need to make sure you find the right team sport—one that emphasizes harmony and cooperation rather than the pressure of being the absolute best, which can stress out a sensitive Six. You also need to make sure you are working within your physical limits. Since you're always pushing yourself for the good of the whole, you're prone to injuries. As for diet, Sixes tend to want to be strong, so you'll be attracted to meats and hearty pasta. Make sure you balance that with "yin" foods, like green, leafy vegetables.

Work

Hardworking and loyal, Sixes make for ideal executives, especially in the number-two slot or in middle management where they still have an authority figure to look up to. You're devoted to the organization and are well guided by your sense of responsibility. You thrive in work environments such as the military, where teamwork offers real benefits and you can rally people together for a common cause. As supervisors, Sixes are able to exercise authority themselves, but they do so in order to get the job done, not as a function of tyranny. A good self-improvement goal for Sixes is to work on practicing the art of mediation, of looking at a subject from all points of view and using your own inner authority instead of looking to a leader for decision making.

Money

Sixes tend to cede control of their money to others whom they perceive as more capable. You need to make sure you carefully question your money managers, however, to make sure your faith in someone else's judgment isn't blind. Make sure you take authority for your own financial situation by becoming well educated about the range of investment options available to you.

How to Recognize a Six

Sixes are hard to spot, since you purposely strive to blend into the crowd. You'll most likely be found in jeans or khakis, shopping at the Gap or Banana Republic.

Famous Sixes

Jason Alexander as George Costanza on *Seinfeld*, Woody Allen, Gordon Liddy, Marilyn Monroe, Mia Farrow

Seven
THE ADVENTURER

1. I enjoy life; I crave excitement.
2. I'm often restless; I can't stand inactivity.
3. I hate it when people beat around the bush.
4. I want to change the world and make it a better place. Call me idealistic.
5. I'm an optimist; I try to get people to see the bright side of things.

It takes just a three-letter word to describe the Seven: fun. Lighthearted, sunny, and playful, you want it all. You take an epicurean approach to life: you want to taste all that the world has to offer. Sevens enjoy exploring new things, and aren't afraid to take risks. Your enthusiasm and pleasure for life is infectious. As a Seven, you tend to remember just the best parts of your childhood. Long ago, you diffused any fear or pain you may have felt by escaping into your prodigious imagination. You tend to start many projects, but rarely see them all through. You're not a good type to come to with problems; Sevens are reluctant to commit to investing the emotional energy in seeing someone else's issues through to resolution. You avoid feeling bored or deprived at all costs, and you don't like confrontation or criticism. It simply spoils your good time.

Strengths

Enthusiastic, highly motivated, generous, fun loving, accomplished, sensual, inspirational, and multitalented

Weaknesses

Superficial, infantile, addictive, escapist, dilettantish, excessive, and manic

Overall Self-improvement Goals

Turn your tendency toward gluttony and distractedness into contentment and focus. You can maximize your enjoyment of life by allowing yourself to experience one thing at a time in depth, rather than flitting from one diversion to another. You enjoy so many things, it's important that you resist the temptation to bite off more than you can chew.

Romance

In romantic relationships, Sevens must learn the virtues of routine, ritual, and commitment. Recognize that tradition has as much value as novelty. An ideal partner for you should thoroughly enjoy humor and the adventure of life, because traveling through life with you will be a thrilling ride.

Friendship

Sevens need to work on fighting their tendency toward inconstancy. It's important to learn to be an all-weather friend, someone who shares in the downs as eagerly as the ups. Ideal friends for you are people who love to have a good time, but can lovingly confront you about your sometimes flighty and impulsive behavior.

Health and Fitness

Sevens love to try everything. You're the first to sign up for rock climbing or kick boxing, activities that are certain to keep you in shape, but only if you stick to one of them with regularity. You also need to watch your diet. Because of your "addictive" personality, you tend to overindulge. It's fine occasionally to sample the most delectable foods, as long as you balance these culinary excursions with a basic diet of considered and disciplined eating.

Work

The entertainment industry is filled with Sevens; you're the best storytellers and writers. In any office, you're the people making it a fun, creative place to work. Your ideal work environment should be flexible, encouraging your ability to use unorthodox methods to accomplish your goals. You will be frustrated in any job that doesn't require creativity; you must learn to sit patiently while others drone on in meetings. Make an effort to develop an appreciation for doing things regularly and thoughtfully. To keep your imagination satisfied, it may help you to have several jobs or projects going at the same time.

Money

Sevens can generate a ton of money because they can sell any-thing—their enthusiasm is that infectious. But as a Seven, you need to be extremely careful about maintaining your savings. Sevens are itinerant gamblers who can easily get carried away playing with their finances as if life were a Monopoly game, and forgetting that they're dealing with actual cash. The occasional gamble is fine, but you need to make sure that you have some-thing that's safe financially, a nest egg that's not risked by the roll of the dice.

How to Recognize a Seven

Your approach to life translates into the clothes you wear: your wardrobe is a quirky fashion playground. You eagerly wear loud colors and enjoy shocking people with your appearance just for the fun of it.

Famous Sevens

Robin Williams, Peter Pan, Hugh Hefner, Goldie Hawn, Steven Spielberg, Jim Carrey, Whoopi Goldberg

Eight

THE ASSERTER

1. I'm a nonconformist and proud of it.
2. I think of myself as powerful.
3. I can't understand why people let others walk all over them.
4. I'll fight for what's right; I love a good argument.
5. I have no problem making decisions.

Eights are the Boss, always the most powerful person in any group or situation. You enjoy being strong and self-reliant; after all, that's the way you'll be able to make the impact you want on the world. Being around Eights is exciting and intense, for they enjoy confrontation and aren't afraid to fight for what they believe in, to stick up for themselves and for friends. As children, many Eights struggled against unfair odds. They survived by standing up to the schoolyard bully, by not crying or showing weakness when their siblings pushed them around. They learned to win by making their enemies back down. But Eights can get abusive if they don't get their way. As an Eight, you're unafraid of open or ugly displays of anger and force, and you need to be in control, to feel dominant at work and at home. Avoiding the slightest sign of weakness, you respect those who stand and fight, and you judge harshly those who don't. You won't easily reveal the smallest chink in your armor. You lead an excessive way of life, and you're routinely criticized for doing too much, being too loud, staying out too late.

Strengths

Enterprising, tough, protective, self-confident, decisive, and courageous

Weaknesses

Exploitative, egomaniacal, authoritative, aggressive, combative, domineering, and territorial

Overall Self-improvement Goals

Turn your need for control into openness and tenderness. Try to be more judicious in the execution of your power, and allow others to see your weaknesses.

Romance

Because Eights find love through being protective and powerful, you need a partner who is sexy and charismatic but not intimidated by shows of anger or strength. As lovers, you should practice the discipline of vulnerable self-disclosure—of revealing yourself to those you love. Remember that it's more important to be close than to be right.

Friendship

As friends, Eights must be willing to reveal their soft underbelly more often. Try to refrain from dramatic but ultimately intimidating displays of your prowess and brawn. You can handle the rough and tough, but you can also, surprisingly, enjoy interactions that are sweet and tender. The best friends for you are people who are self-assured, confident, and can run with the wolves.

Health and Fitness

Look out, Arnold Schwarzenegger: Eights enjoy weight lifting and muscle building because they desire external evidence of their strength and aggressiveness. It's important for you to develop your soft muscles as well, by doing regular stretching and lengthening exercises. You also tend to bring your aggression to the table, where you eat with gusto and wolf down your food. Instead, try to eat as slowly as possible, concentrating on eating as a meditative process.

Work

Eights are textbook entrepreneurs and businesspeople; you've got the strong stomach to endure, and even enjoy, the roller coaster of politics and high finance. You should be in a job that utilizes your power and leadership abilities, but doesn't permit you to rule by intimidation or manipulation. You can be a magnanimous and inclusive leader, provided you develop an "impartial witness" capacity to see both sides. For the best exercise of your power, try to develop temperance and learn to listen to the little guy. Make an effort to see the weakest member of the team as your secret teacher about the effectiveness of diversity and consensus.

Money

Money is power, especially to Eights, so you tend to get carried away with aggressive manipulation of your finances, and those of others. It's one thing to risk your own portfolio—you've got the stomach for it—but it's not fair to expect others to enjoy the ride, too. Remember that money can also be a tool of philanthropy, not just a tool for achieving power over people.

How to Recognize an Eight

Power lunches, three-piece business suits—that's classic Eight style. Your clothes say "Take notice of me" through expensive fabrics and sophisticated design, not through bold colors or loud fabrics. Eights can be found sitting at the head of a table, never along the side, and they never sit with their backs to the door—that's a poor position for self-defense.

Famous Eights

Marlon Brando as Vito Corleone in *The Godfather*, Rush Limbaugh, John Wayne, Donald Trump, Saddam Hussein, Bette Midler, Barbra Streisand, Barbara Walters

Nine

THE PEACEMAKER

1. I prefer simply walking away to confronting somebody.
2. I dislike change.
3. I'm sensitive and don't like being criticized.
4. I don't make decisions easily; I always see both sides of any situation.
5. I like to listen to other people.

"Give Peace a Chance" could be the Nine's theme song. Your driving force is peace and harmony, which you always want to achieve, no matter the cost. You're an ideal counselor and negotiator; you can always get all sides to sit down at the table and hash things out. But your ability to see all sides can translate into obsessive ambivalence and indecision. Faced with conflict or tension that you can't resolve, you'll tune out with whatever drug is at hand—food, alcohol, television. You'll do whatever you can to ignore the problem, even get lazy and procrastinate. As a child, you often felt overshadowed by siblings or ignored; you learned to tune out when your parents argued. As an adult, you're not fond of change or disruption in the routine, since you find comfort in rules and tradition. You put the needs of others ahead of your own; in fact, you're probably more aware of what others want than what you want yourself.

Strengths

Receptive, responsive, nurturing, flexible, patient, stable, and comforting

Weaknesses

Spaced out, passive, painfully self-effacing, complacent, passive-aggressive, and disengaged

Overall Self-improvement Goals

To let go of your inertia and complacency, develop self-awareness, and gain confidence in the power of your own convictions

Romance

In romance, Nines must remember that while peace is necessary for stability, conflict is a healthy sign of a maturing, evolving relationship. It's important for you to grow to be a more emotionally awake, vital partner. You need a partner who can appreciate and value your selflessness, but who is also deeply interested in what's lying hidden underneath your calm and accommodating exterior.

Friendship

You hesitate to rock the boat, but you should still strive to be as honest as you can be about your true likes and dislikes. You should seek friends who will treasure the relationship without taking your good nature for granted. Although you'll never stop offering them the shirt off your back or the last dollar in your wallet, you'll find satisfaction in knowing that they value you for who you are rather than what you give them.

Health and Fitness

Nines fall victim easily to sloth. If you exercise at all, you're drawn to leg lifts and passive activities you can do while watching television. But it's critical that you do some exercise that will stimulate your cardiovascular system, something that makes your heart pump faster. The more aerobic the activity, the better.

Nines tend to be drawn to an escapist's high, so you should make sure to engage in your food and exercise, rather than using them to space out. You love foods like chocolate that give you a feeling of euphoria; instead, try to eat spicier foods that warm up the body and help you stay alert.

Work

Nines are ideal arbitrators or diplomats, the peacekeepers in any office. You're great in situations that require levelheaded, fair, dispassionate expertise. Nines are kind, good listeners, who bring out the best in everyone—you make others feel that they can keep going even when they're exhausted. But even though you're the kings and queens of diplomacy, you have to be willing to take a stand and defend your opinions when necessary.

Money

You need to get a clear sense of what your budget is, to be realistic about what your money goals are. Because people like you so much, you have no problem getting jobs or making money, but because you have trouble making decisions, you need some expert help coming up with a financial plan. You function best with some type of financial monitoring system, so you can keep track of your intake and outgo and regulate your finances.

How to Recognize a Nine

Nines tend to talk slowly and always have some kind of saga to tell—you like to draw people in. You're also pleasing to look at: your clothes are alluring, soft, shapely. Others feel drawn to you because the way you look and move feels friendly and inviting.

Famous Nines

Bill Clinton, Marge Simpson, Ronald Reagan

Best and Worst Matches

One
Best Match: Seven
Worst Match: Four, Eight

Two
Best Match: Four
Worst Match: Eight

Three
Best Match: Six
Worst Match: Nine

Four
Best Match: One
Worst Match: Two, Five

Five
Best Match: Eight
Worst Match: Seven

Six
Best Match: Nine
Worst Match: Three

Seven
Best Match: Five
Worst Match: One

Eight

Best Match: Two

Worst Match: Five

Nine

Best Match: Three

Worst Match: Six

5

Ayurveda

ased on a system of medicine that's been around for more than five thousand years, Ayurveda ranks as the oldest personality test in our book. A Sanskrit word meaning the science or knowledge (*veda*) of life (*ayu*), Ayurveda is a holistic, whole-body system of healing. Its basic principle is that well-being is created when the self is nourished physically, spiritually, and emotionally. According to Ayurveda, everything we do—what we eat, where we live, how we sleep, how active we are, as well as how we interact with our surroundings, our environment, and each other—affects our health.

In the Ayurvedic system, the body is composed of the five elements in nature: space, air, fire, water, and earth. These elements organize themselves into three body types called *doshas*: Vata, Pitta, and Kapha. The three doshas govern all of the functions of the body, controlling both our physical and psychological behaviors.

Though everyone possesses some characteristics of each of the three doshas, we are born having a *primary* dosha that is most influential in our lives. The amount of each dosha that we possess in relation to the others then creates our complete personality. Your primary dosha determines how you look, how you move, how you talk, what you eat (and crave), even how you prefer to burn it off. Learning to recognize your dosha gives you a valuable tool for regulating your weight, maintaining better health, and identifying the activities that will be deeply rewarding for you. Your dosha makes you who you are—and understanding yourself offers a path to a more satisfying, fulfilling life.

Balance among the three doshas is key. If one dosha gets *too* dominant within us, we can run into trouble, physically or emotionally. Any kind of imbalance—caused by unhealthy habits, a bad diet, or simply the stresses of modern life—depletes our immune system, leaving us vulnerable to sickness and disease. When the doshas are in harmony, though, the body functions normally. We have plenty of energy, and we enjoy good health. Every experience we have—sounds, sights, smells, tastes—influences the delicate balance of the doshas, positively and negatively. Ingesting too many toxins, for example, may disrupt the balance, but it can be righted again by eating healthful meals suited to your body type, along with getting regular exercise and practicing relaxation techniques like meditation.

Since Ayurveda is at its core a system of medicine, we'll be emphasizing healthful diet and fitness habits in this chapter. What you eat and how you exercise is crucial to keeping your dosha in balance. Some general Ayurvedic tips on eating: Don't eat when you're upset or rushed. Don't talk while chewing, or gobble down your food. Eat only when you're hungry, and try to leave the table with your stomach partially empty. Limit your intake of cold drinks while you eat—the body digests best at room temperature.

Another important Ayurvedic principle involves the power of taste. Ayurvedic practitioners believe that "like increases like"—meaning that experiencing a particular taste will provoke a similar, related emotional or physical effect within the body. All foods can be divided into six tastes, and you can learn to regulate your doshas by combining foods of all these tastes into your daily diet. The six tastes are: pungent (chilis, peppers); sweet (sugar, dairy, carbohydrates, meats); sour (citrus fruits, tomatoes, cheese); salty (soy sauce, anchovies); bitter (green leafy vegetables, tea and coffee, chocolate); astringent (beans, lentils). We'll explain later how each of these tastes affects the three doshas.

How do you know which is your primary dosha? Each manifests itself through certain physical characteristics. Read through the physical description lists for each dosha, and note which one contains the most characteristics that describe you. You'll probably see parts of yourself in all three, but you should select the dosha that *best* captures your physical and psychological profile. There may be a close second, another dosha that also seems to represent you. That's your secondary dosha. It, too, plays a role in your overall health and well-being, having an impact of its own as well as modifying your primary dosha. For your best overall self-portrait, keep in mind the advice offered for both your primary and secondary doshas.

Vata

Physique
Thin, slim, and lanky; little muscular definition; rarely gain weight

Skin
Cool, rough, dry

Hair

Dark, curly, dry

Eyes

Small; dark brown, gray, or slate blue

Sleep Habits

Don't require much sleep; sleep lightly and awaken easily

Appetite

Irregular, eat quickly

Mood

Nervous, anxious, creative

Energy Level

Inconsistent bursts of energy; poor physical stamina

Health Problems

Irregular digestion, bloating, constipation

Governed by the elements of space and air, Vatas are thin and light in appearance, and quick in thought, speech, and action. You're constantly in motion physically (you've got high kinetic energy) and psychologically (your moods can fluctuate wildly). As a Vata, your high energy generates tremendous creativity, but it can also generate anxiety and worry as well. When the Vata force is in balance, you're lively, imaginative, and enthusiastic. When it's out of balance, you're prone to stress and insomnia.

Strengths

Quick, agile, and active

Weaknesses
Fearful, undependable, and scattered

Motive
The most ethereal of the three doshas, you want to be appreciated for your light, adaptive qualities, but at the same time, you need to feel secure and centered. You should still reach for the stars, but try to remember to keep your feet on the ground.

Taking Care of Yourself
A Vata's tendency to do everything quickly also applies to eating habits. You need to make a deliberate effort to slow down at mealtimes, to be aware of your digestion, and to eat in a thoughtful, mindful manner. Be sure to sit down while eating; never eat on the run. The Vata force is increased by pungent, bitter, and astringent tastes, and decreased by sweet, sour, and salty foods, so when you feel yourself getting too distracted, you can ground yourself with sweet, sour, and salty foods. For fitness, focus on aerobic exercise that moves energy from your intellect into your limbs and body. Exercise should be regular, gentle, and above all, moderate—like swimming or yoga.

Your Love Life
Vatas are looking for an exciting and stimulating relationship that also provides a sense of home. Because you can be flighty, you need a partner who can anchor you without weighing you down—a fear you're likely to run from as fast as you can. You need to learn to appreciate the security and stability that love can provide, while offering your partner the benefit of your uniquely imaginative point of view. Though you thrill in speeding toward the future, remember that others don't always like to

move so fast. You should be willing to go slowly when needed and take stock in the present. Learn to enjoy the process of building a loving, lasting relationship.

Your Friendships

You need invigorating friendships that make you feel alive; your ideal friends are people who appreciate your energy and creativity, and who often have plenty of their own. You can tend to feel overwhelmed by the daily demands of life, so you need friends who can support you without overburdening you emotionally or feeling threatened by you. You can return the favor simply by being consistent—faithful, loyal, and constant. Your friends need to know that despite your flightiness, you can be there for them when they need you.

Your Career

Work isn't the Vata's strong suit; you've got too many big ideas floating around in your head to be content to sit still. You'd wither in a nine-to-five office job. Instead, you thrive on work that includes travel—pilot or travel writer, perhaps—and the arts and culture. You should seek out an unusual position that allows for a varied daily routine. To achieve balance, though, you need to be willing to stay in one place when needed, and focus on one topic for as long as necessary to get the job done.

Your Finances

Given the Vata's innate flightiness, you are prone to spending money too quickly on attractive trifles, throwing it away on questionable investment schemes. Learn to balance your desire to spend with a future-oriented goal structure for saving. Since you tend to rush through things, enlist the help of an advisor who'll be patient enough to keep your checkbook balanced.

Famous Vatas

Gwyneth Paltrow, Goldie Hawn, Uma Thurman, Andy Warhol, Richard Gere, Robert Redford

Pitta

Physique

Medium; good muscular development; gain and lose weight easily

Skin

Warm, oily; sunburns and breaks out easily

Hair

Light, straight, fine

Eyes

Bright blue, light brown

Sleep Habits

Require sleep; sleep soundly

Appetite

Good appetite; need to eat regularly; can eat large quantities

Mood

Impulsive; strong-willed; easily irritated and angered; perfectionistic

Energy Level

Moderate energy levels; average stamina

Health Problems

Indigestion and heartburn

The Pitta dosha is characterized by heat and intensity. You're sharp, determined, and intense—you have a strong, booming voice and you speak assertively. Your memory is quick; you're a critical thinker and skilled debater. As a matter of fact, you often find yourself in debates—even arguments—with others, since you're very opinionated and you get impatient and irritated easily. You're very organized and efficient, but that means you're prone to perfectionism because you have little tolerance for errors. When the Pitta force is in balance, you're courageous, sincere, and warm; when it's out of balance, you're judgmental, intolerant, jealous, critical, and aggressive.

Strengths

Intelligent, assertive, bold, and directed

Weaknesses

Angry, irritable, fanatic, and opinionated

Motive

To learn to be generous, compassionate, and patient with others

Taking Care of Yourself

Your primary goal is to bring dispassion to your eating habits and fitness routine. The same passion that drives you in work and relationships can also lead you to overeating, or not eating at all. The Pitta force is increased by pungent, sour, and salty tastes, and it is decreased by sweet, bitter, and astringent foods. So you should stay away from spicy foods and eat more dark green foods, which will calm your system. Pittas need to get regular exercise to release a lot of physical energy in a short amount of time. While you need an activity more challenging than a long walk, you should also avoid competitive sports, which will simply serve to generate more emotion than you can work off. (Pittas are likely to endlessly recount triumphs—and wallow in mistakes—long after the game has ended.) Instead, try aerobics classes, bike riding, or a Stairmaster. And after your workout, be sure to cool down with some kind of meditation that brings your energy level back into balance.

Your Love Life

Though Pittas are looking for a hot, passionate, intensely engaged connection, you also need to be tolerant of the inevitably dull and routine parts of relationships. Passion—the life force of the Pitta—is only one aspect of a healthy relationship, and it tends to wax and wane, especially as you get to know the foibles of your partner (and vice versa). To avoid being doomed to a lifetime of short-lived romances that burn out quickly, you must learn to appreciate the everyday activities that provide the building blocks of long-lasting intimate relationships.

Your Friendships

Pittas like to argue, but your friends shouldn't take your anger seriously. They'll learn to wait out your temper, because it fades away quickly. You need friends who are good-natured and unafraid of your intensity. Since you can occasionally come on too strong, in order to be a better friend yourself, you should learn to channel the frustration and anger you often feel into problem solving and cooperation. Don't be so quick to jump on a friend and launch into one of your trademark tirades. A helpful tip for Pittas: Count to a hundred before expressing any anger or criticism.

Your Career

You thrive in competitive atmospheres where you can exercise your intellectual and emotional muscle. You'd make a great athlete or politician—arenas ruled by the principle "survival of the fittest." You're fond of leadership positions, in which you can usually excel. But you must learn that victory isn't the only measure of success. You can also find value in the service and support of others.

Your Finances

Given the Pitta's abundant intelligence, you tend to earn money well and show common sense in managing it. But with your short fuse, you're prone to dropping a lot of cash wildly in a burst of emotion—going on a mad shopping spree after a confrontation with a partner, for example, or buying several rounds of drinks for everyone in the bar in a victory celebration. You should stay away from gambling in any form—it's likely to evoke an emotional response in you that you'll soon lose control of. Instead of using money to fulfill an emotional need, look to your partner and friends for support. And make sure they hold your wallet.

Famous Pittas

Barbra Streisand, Madonna, Sigourney Weaver, Nicole Kidman, Demi Moore, Jack Nicholson, Robert De Niro, Mike Tyson

Kapha

Physique

Large, round build; good muscular development; gain weight easily

Skin

Cool, smooth, moist, soft

Hair

Thick, wavy, dark

Eyes

Large, brown

Sleep Habits

Like to sleep; sleep deeply

Appetite

Steady appetite; eat slowly; enjoy food

Mood

Calm, tranquil, compassionate, thorough

Energy Level

Steady energy levels; good endurance but lethargic

Health Problems

Nasal or sinus congestion; asthma

The elements of water and earth rule over Kaphas, imbuing them with a strong sense of substance and support. They are steady and tolerant, leading a relaxed, slow-paced lifestyle. As a Kapha, you tend to talk slowly and speak only when you have something to say. You also learn slowly, but you don't forget easily. You're slow to anger, and you seldom lose your temper. You're well organized and thorough, and you always see things through to their conclusion. When the Kapha force is in balance, you're stable, nurturing, and loving; when it's out of balance, you're resistant to change, greedy, controlling, lethargic, and prone to weight gain.

Strengths

Reliable, loyal, and trustworthy

Weaknesses

Retentive, monotonous, stubborn, and insecure

Motive

To take more risks and to express yourself more. Don't be afraid to stand up for yourself—challenges are scary, but they can also be instructive.

Taking Care of Yourself

The most lethargic of the three doshas (the same force that promotes stability can also act against you), Kaphas need to invigorate their bodies religiously to avoid weight gain. Though you don't really like to get up in the morning, try to force yourself to stick to a regular habit of getting out of bed as soon as you wake up, rather than feeding your lethargy by repeatedly hitting the snooze button. And once you're up, launch into a regular, vigorous fitness program to get your metabolism moving at the start of the day. Stay away from sweet, sour, and salty foods that stimulate your dosha, and eat more pungent, bitter, and astringent foods. Proteins and spices will speed up your metabolism and make your body want to get up and go. Fight your Kapha-driven urge to sit on the couch all day with a bowl of ice cream—and get moving!

Your Love Life

Your ideal partners are thoughtful, contemplative people who can also offer you just the right dose of spicy unpredictability.

You need your boat to be rocked every once in a while. As a Kapha, you must learn to infuse your relationships with a sense of adventure, without worrying that your life will be destroyed as a result. Because you cling to stability, you must learn to see that relationships are also an opportunity for growth, spiritually and emotionally. People change over time, but that doesn't mean they grow apart. You need to give your relationships room to grow and adapt accordingly.

Your Friendships

Caring, attentive listeners, Kaphas are loyal and devoted in their relationships. So you want friends who are stimulating and easy-going; friends who will cherish and engage you, but also not take you for granted or drag you into a daily emotional soap opera, since you're uncomfortable with wild swings of emotion. To be a better friend yourself, work on being more flexible and compromising. Life doesn't always go according to plan. Be willing to ride the wave—every once in a while.

Your Career

As you do in other areas of your life, you seek stability at work. You don't have the stomach for the ups and downs of the stock market or any field hallmarked by high job turnover and ruthless competition. Instead, you want to feel that you're making some kind of aesthetic contribution to the world, that you're involved in promoting beauty and harmony. You work best in atmospheres that deal with art and creativity, such as photography, filmmaking, and decorating. Though Kaphas don't like to call attention to themselves, you can be more successful at work by speaking up more and sharing your opinions and ideas. And since you tend to be rather dogmatic, you also need to make an effort to be more receptive to the opinions of others.

Your Finances

Because Kaphas need to feel safe and comfortable at all times, you're a good saver who sleeps better at night knowing you've got a sizable savings account socked away. That means, though, that you may be prone to being greedy and miserly, holding on to your money too tightly. You'd benefit from confronting this fear by taking modest financial risks—say, in the stock market—that will probably offer greater financial reward than stuffing cash into your mattress.

Famous Kaphas

Rosie O'Donnell, Oprah Winfrey, Janeane Garofalo, Roseanne, John Goodman, Rush Limbaugh, Marlon Brando

Best and Worst Matches

Vata
Best Match: Kapha
Worst Match: Pitta

Pitta
Best Match: Pitta
Worst Match: Vata

Kapha
Best Match: Pitta
Worst Match: Kapha

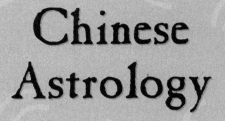

Chinese Astrology

Chinese astrology is a system of horoscopes over five thousand years old. Like its Western counterpart, Chinese astrology is divided into twelve signs. But rather than monthly, these signs appear yearly, one following the other. The twelve signs, all named for animals, are said to shape the personality of everyone born during that year. You may develop other habits and traits as you go through life, but in Chinese lore, your birth sign reveals "the animal that hides in your heart." It's who you are in your soul.

According to legend, before the Lord Buddha left the earth, he summoned all the world's animals to come to him. Only twelve answered his call, so as a reward, he named a year after each in the order they arrived: Rat, Ox, Tiger, Rabbit, Dragon, Snake, Horse, Sheep, Monkey, Rooster, Dog, and Pig. The Chinese calendar then revolves around this twelve-year cycle. Those who share the animal sign of the current year can usually expect good fortune while their animal is reigning.

What Is Your Sign?

All you need to know to determine your Chinese astrology sign is the year of your birth.

Rat: 1900, 1912, 1924, 1936, 1948, 1960, 1972, 1984, 1996
Ox: 1901, 1913, 1925, 1937, 1949, 1961, 1973, 1985, 1997
Tiger: 1902, 1914, 1926, 1938, 1950, 1962, 1974, 1986, 1998
Rabbit: 1903, 1915, 1927, 1939, 1951, 1963, 1975, 1987, 1999
Dragon: 1904, 1916, 1928, 1940, 1952, 1964, 1976, 1988
Snake: 1905, 1917, 1929, 1941, 1953, 1965, 1977, 1989
Horse: 1906, 1918, 1930, 1942, 1954, 1966, 1978, 1990
Goat: 1907, 1919, 1931, 1943, 1955, 1967, 1979, 1991
Monkey: 1908, 1920, 1932, 1944, 1956, 1968, 1980, 1992
Rooster: 1909, 1921, 1933, 1945, 1957, 1969, 1981, 1993
Dog: 1910, 1922, 1934, 1946, 1958, 1970, 1982, 1994
Pig: 1911, 1923, 1935, 1947, 1959, 1971, 1983, 1995

Rat

You're the entrepreneurs of the Chinese astrological system. You're hardworking and industrious, but also incredibly resourceful and clever. You know what it takes to get ahead, and you're willing to do whatever is necessary to get there. You live by the twin driving forces of power and money.

Strengths
Charming, deft, strategic, magnetic, shrewd, and expressive

Weaknesses

Aggressive, narrow-minded, restless, anxious, and conniving

Overall Self-improvement Goals

To work toward the good of humanity and those you love instead of solely for your own self in the pursuit of material acquisitions

Your Love Life

Those born in the year of the Rat tend to be loyal, devoted partners. You're too pragmatic to be a head-over-heels romantic, but you can be sensual and loving to the right person. Your ideal partner is someone who is trustworthy and straightforward, but who at the same time is also a bit mysterious to pique your curiosity and keep your interest, because you're easily bored. Rats tend to be their own worst enemy in relationships because they don't like to share. So don't be afraid to open up and reveal your true feelings to your partner.

Your Friendships

Rats are party animals. They know how to work a scene and make the most of the attention they get. As a Rat, you're well known and popular; everyone seems to know your name. But these people tend to be mostly acquaintances rather than real friends. You probably have only a few truly close friends, and they tend to be like you, movers and shakers who can get things done. Even though you revere and cherish these friends and consider them to be like family, you tend to keep your problems to yourself and rarely confide in anyone. It's an uphill battle getting to know a Rat, because you're very protective of your inner thoughts and feelings. Try to give more of yourself, to scurry away less to your rathole when you're feeling threatened, and to be more honest with those close to you about your deepest needs and expectations.

Your Career

Your entrepreneurial skills serve you well in the business world. You're a natural leader; you'd do well as a politician, executive, salesperson, or diplomat. But you're not always easy to work with because Rats are extremely perfectionistic and demand nothing but the best from themselves and others. You'd suffocate in a job that didn't allow you any freedom to explore; you thrive on adrenaline and the fast pace of business. You need work that utilizes your shrewd intelligence and allows you flexible conditions (no nine to five!). And of course, you'd prefer to be the boss. To be more successful at work, here are a few tips: Try to share more of what you know with your colleagues (stop being so stealthy!). Hold yourself accountable for your mistakes—as you do your co-workers. And give credit where credit is due. You'd expect as much from your boss.

Your Finances

Because money brings the status you crave, you appreciate the value of a dollar. Your entrepreneurial streak is thrilled by the challenge of wheeling and dealing, and since Rats are conservators, you know how to hoard your treasures. But even as you salt away your profits, try to be more generous to yourself from time to time. Let yourself enjoy the fruits of your considerable labors.

Health and Fitness

Rats are often so busy that they don't let themselves relax—they've probably forgotten how. But all that stress can wreak havoc on the body. To release tension, you need to do exercise that helps you breathe and stretch: try hiking, walking, yoga, and Pilates—anything that offers you the opportunity to relax your muscles. When it comes to eating, you tend to nibble here and there, which may not provide you with all the nutrients you need. Make yourself sit down and eat your meals contemplatively. "Rooted" foods (potatoes and protein), as opposed to spicy foods, will help calm your active system.

How to Recognize a Rat

Think Alec Baldwin. Rats are sharp dressers, perfectly pressed and ready to go anywhere, clothed in an expensive wardrobe in keeping with their prestige-seeking nature.

Famous Rats

Antonio Banderas, Hugh Grant, David Duchovny, Gwyneth Paltrow, Cameron Diaz, Sean Penn, Prince Charles, Jimmy Carter, Marlon Brando, Charlton Heston

Ox

People born in the year of the Ox tend to be firmly grounded, with their feet planted solidly in the present. As an Ox, you have little patience with the trends and fads of today; instead, your values are rooted in the past. You tend to be old-fashioned in your philosophy and outlook, and the fast pace of our contemporary world makes you anxious. You're thoughtful and contemplative, reluctant to let your hair down, but you've also got a fierce temper that makes you act rashly and impulsively at times. Though that temper doesn't flare up often, when it does, those on the receiving end won't soon forget it.

Strengths

Honest, practical, steadfast, diligent, and enduring

Weaknesses

Obstinate, lethargic, depressive, dogmatic, and stubborn. Once you've made up your mind, nothing will change it.

Overall Self-improvement Goals

To become more flexible and tolerant of the vicissitudes of life. Remember to let yourself enjoy a good time.

Your Love Life

When Oxes fall in love, they fall in love forever. But they don't do it easily or often. As an Ox, you're not overly sentimental, but you are deeply devoted to the object of your affections. You need someone who can fire you up and challenge you—someone who's independent, successful, and high-spirited. To be a better partner, you should try to be more willing to accommodate your mate—not everything has to go your way. With your partner, make an effort to create innovative and varied romantic rituals that will keep the spark of love alive between you.

Your Friendships

Oxes aren't very social or outgoing; at parties, they're likely to be found sitting in a quiet corner. But you do have many friends who flock to you for your remarkable capacity for patience and caring. You're the best friend anyone could ever have. But it's much easier for you to listen to others' problems than to share your own, and so you often feel that even those closest to you fail to understand you. Your best friends are those who can help you lighten up and be less stubborn by reminding you that change is healthy and life can sometimes be absurd. To be a better friend yourself, you need to become more open. Push yourself to be more social, and stop keeping to yourself. You're desperately afraid of conflict, but if it does surface, remember that if you work through it, your friendships might be strengthened by surmounting such a challenge.

Your Career

Oxes aren't the innovators who come up with new ideas to revolutionize the world, but they are incredibly devoted workers, and that can be just as valuable. The downside is that you tend to be workaholics, putting in long hours and seldom taking vacations. You have high standards, and you're a harsh judge of people who don't meet them. Even though you tend to get stuck in your particular way of doing things, you're well respected as a leader, and as a colleague you're well liked for your devotion to your work and your patient demeanor. You don't mind working backstage, basking in the reflected glow of the star. You're happy working in a large organization, but you can also be just as content working on your own, as long as you have clear goals: You'd do well as an architect, engineer, or real estate agent. You can happily spend hours on end tweaking details and solving problems, so it's important to make yourself take occasional breaks to keep your mind fresh and energized. You also need to learn to appreciate the social aspects of work and to be more carefree and relaxed in your work environment. A little chatter around the office cooler won't destroy your productivity.

Your Finances

Oxes tend to make small but important financial successes throughout their careers, and their bank accounts prove it. But you needn't—and shouldn't—be satisfied with slow but steady growth in your income. Take an occasional risk with an IPO or a recommended stock tip that has the potential of great reward.

Health and Fitness

As an Ox, you don't know how to relax—even your fitness routine is likely to be heavy on steady aerobic exercise that exhausts you. Instead, you need to do routines that calm you and lengthen and elasticize your muscles, instead of bulking you up. Try yoga, Pilates, or tai chi. Given your tendency to gain weight easily, make sure to stay away from large meals heavy in fat and starches.

How to Recognize an Ox

Oxes aren't known for making shocking fashion statements. Rather, they blend in because of their traditional conservative tastes. While there's something to be said for classic styles, a bit more flair and variety wouldn't hurt you.

Famous Oxen

Meg Ryan, Bill Cosby, Jack Nicholson, Sigourney Weaver, Meryl Streep, George Clooney, Neve Campbell, Jane Fonda, Robert Redford

Tiger

Tigers are born adventurers. Nothing scares you; you live for each next challenge, addicted to excitement and the rush of adrenaline. You're a daring fighter, ready to defend your own rights at all costs and those of the people you love. Your courage and passion are infectious, making you a natural leader. You're driven by a need to be in control, to call the shots. You prefer being obeyed rather than obeying someone else. But you have a tendency to rush headlong into every pursuit and so you need to learn the meaning—and appreciate the benefits—of moderation.

Strengths

Magnetic, passionate, powerful, fearless, and courageous

Weaknesses

Impatient, emotional, tempestuous, unpredictable, and overconfident

Overall Self-improvement Goals

To learn to stop and smell the roses as you speed along on your life's journey. Try to live in the moment instead of constantly looking ahead to the next conquest.

Your Love Life

Tigers are die-hard, passionate lovers. You fall in love quickly and easily, but you tend to get too intense about it, becoming territorial and possessive—often stifling the object of your affection. You need a partner who can be a stabilizing influence, who can be very patient and responsive to your whims. You'll have better luck in love if you try to quell your impatience. Be true to your lover and demonstrate your commitment—instead of always looking over your mate's shoulder to see whom you might be missing.

Your Friendships

You're an ideal friend because you'll eagerly and without question take a buddy's side against the bad guys—Tigers are valuable allies because of their ample power. You tend to seek out friends who are as wild and exciting as you are, but you should also surround yourself with people who can help you develop a more temperate approach to life. Try to be less hasty in your judgments of others, and make a conscious effort to listen to what your friends have to say instead of only focusing on your own needs.

Your Career

Simply put, Tigers like to work. You're driven, forceful, and you thrive on stress. You especially enjoy working alone, because you're always in a hurry and you'd rather not have to wait for anyone to catch up to you. Tigers need to be in entrepreneurial situations where their bright minds and quick ideas can earn them a lot of power and respect quickly. You have little patience for working "within the system." Ideal careers for Tigers are pilot, advertising executive, explorer—anything that allows you to push the limits. Tigers change careers often and have a long résumé of interesting occupations, so don't worry if you have trouble landing in the right job. No matter what your position or title, you'll always do your work with enthusiasm and efficiency—as long as you remember to try to stay within the expectations of authority.

Your Finances

Your penchant for taking risks makes you a natural player in the stock market. Your fortune has probably already risen and fallen several times, and it will undoubtedly do so again. Your tendency to go to extremes may have even caused you to go bankrupt, but there's no need to worry. With Tigers, the moment the money is gone, more just seems to show up, thanks to your endless innovative ideas. Even so, it's not fiscally wise to run through money like a mouse through cheese. Try to think of money as a reservoir, and learn to value and conserve your particular pool. During times of plenty, be sure to put away a small but sizable sum regularly. Then forget about it. Don't rush out to invest or spend it, just because you have it.

Health and Fitness

Given the Tiger's penchant for adventure, you're probably in very good shape. You were one of the first to try activities like in-line skating, mountain biking, snowboarding, and hang gliding when they were first invented. To balance your need for speed, though, try to incorporate some slow-moving routines into your life, like tai chi and meditation. The same goes for eating. Tigers like hot, spicy food, and they like it fast. To save yourself heartburn and weight gain, remember: everything in moderation.

How to Recognize a Tiger

Tigers are seductive and attractive, and they dress as though they know it. You're the innovative upstarts of fashion, wearing daring, wild clothes to get the attention you crave.

Famous Tigers

Rosie O'Donnell, Jodie Foster, Tom Cruise, Demi Moore, Martin Short, Leonardo DiCaprio, Phil Collins, Queen Elizabeth, Stevie Wonder

Rabbit

Rabbits have an imaginative, sensitive soul that makes them very popular among the other "animals." You enjoy good company, and you offer a calming presence to those around you. Rabbits aren't easily provoked. In fact, you really dislike arguments of any kind, and to avoid conflict, you tend to bottle up your feelings without sharing them, shunning close emotional involvement. While you know how to have a good time, you live in fear of doing anything rashly. You will never begin a new job, project, or even a relationship, without evaluating and weighing all aspects.

Strengths

Elegant, friendly, artistic, ethical, compassionate, and wise

Weaknesses

Eccentric, fearful, neurotic, insecure, and cautious

Overall Self-improvement Goals

To be more comfortable taking stands and expressing opinions

Your Love Life

Given their romantic, sweet, faithful nature, Rabbits never lack for lovers and can be a great partner for anyone. You seek out lovers who, like you, are peaceful, harmonious, and sensitive. Rabbits disdain fits of uncontrolled passion and grand shows of emotion. As a result, they often keep their feelings so tucked away that their partners may never really know how they feel. You'd benefit by learning to become more revealing of yourself. Instead of being afraid to express your opinions, share whatever is on your mind. Ask for help when you need it.

Your Friendships

Rabbits far prefer the calm status quo of a longtime friendship to a passionate romantic commitment that quickly dies out. Your friendships, therefore, tend to be far more valuable to you than your romantic relationships. You seek out friends who share your sense of propriety, but you should consider stretching your horizons by befriending people who will loosen you up and introduce you to new worlds. In order to achieve real intimacy, you need to let down your guard and deepen your friendships by letting others know what's in your heart and mind.

Your Career

Rabbits work best alone and for themselves, since they find structured corporate offices stifling. You will thrive in a position that offers a lot of privacy to do your work, but also a lot of responsibility: doctor, teacher, counselor, or social worker. Because of your tendency to bury your ideas and opinions, you can become a more highly valued employee by making an effort to be more of a team player, sharing your thought processes aloud, and enjoying an open exchange of ideas.

Your Finances

Detail-oriented Rabbits appreciate the precision of the financial world, so it's no surprise that you're fairly successful in this area. Rabbits have the ability to make lots of money, and they're pretty good about saving it. Because you tend toward being risk averse, you need to keep in mind that a little risk can occasionally bring big rewards.

Health and Fitness

Rabbits are prone to bursts of energy, so you're easily bored by the monotony of running on a treadmill or climbing a Stairmaster to nowhere. Instead, find a routine that offers a challenge and a clear goal: horseback riding, sailing, or hiking through the wilderness. These activities will require you to tap into your innate resourcefulness. When it comes to diet, if left to your own devices, you'd graze in the same four or five foods, day after day.

In order to get all the nutrients you need, be sure to bring some variety to your diet by trying new cuisines and experimenting with different flavors.

How to Recognize a Rabbit

Rabbits have exquisite, discerning taste, so while you probably won't stand out in a crowd, there's no mistaking your impeccable, unassailable style up close.

Famous Rabbits

Brad Pitt, Johnny Depp, Drew Barrymore, Kate Winslet, Helen Hunt, Nicolas Cage, Sting, Francis Ford Coppola, Quentin Tarantino

Dragon

Dragons are the only mythical creature of Chinese astrology—and for good reason. No animal exists in real life that captures your dynamism, grandeur, and color. Simply put, you're over the top—and you know it. Dragons are the master of ceremonies, ever at the center of attention. There's no blending into the crowd or lurking at the sidelines for you; you're far too confident and feisty to sit quietly. Aggressive and determined, you go after what you want with the full force of your considerable mental and physical powers—unsurprisingly, you're intolerant of failure and rejection. Born believing in the force of your own perfection, as a Dragon, you don't take kindly to anything, or anyone, standing in your path.

Strengths

Confident, imaginative, gifted, energetic, charismatic, and naturally regal

Weaknesses

Overbearing, tyrannical, moody, snobbish, and inflexible

Overall Self-improvement Goals

To tame your fiery power. You tend to be too outspoken, so you need to learn to control your temper and rein in your ego. Dragons have such a strong life force that they often forget to acknowledge the presence and contributions of others. You need to remember that true power isn't in the hands of the individual; rather, it comes from connection with others.

Your Love Life

Dragon women tend to be surrounded by admirers; Dragon men find that women flock to their side wherever they go. You're never disappointed in your search for love—it always seems to find you. As a Dragon, you enjoy being worshiped, but you're better off with a more powerful partner who can keep up with you and match your fire with fire. Otherwise you'll fall in and out of love endlessly. While you're notoriously commitment phobic, the right person can get you to settle down. You have a tendency to rule the roost, which your partner can become weary of, so try to empathize instead of tyrannize. To avoid overwhelming your mate, make sure you occasionally open your heart instead of always breathing fire and passion.

Your Friendships

Extremely popular and social Dragons thrive on surrounding themselves with others. You're good to your friends, especially those who show you constant devotion and the worship to which you feel you're entitled. Dragons don't like being overshadowed, so you need friends who are equally influential but more practical and flexible than you are. You have a tendency to be self-involved, so it's important for you to work on being more sensitive and caring to your friends. You may not innately recognize that friendship needs to be a two-way street, so remember to make yourself available to others when they need you.

Your Career

Dragons need to be in charge, in a position of absolute power— that's the only place where they'll be happy. You feed on the adrenaline and authority of being at the top. But your big ideas are often impractical, so sometimes you need to be reined in by your employees. They know to do so with caution, since you hate orders—except, of course, for those you give yourself. Ideal careers for you are those that let you strut your stuff, like a lawyer in a courtroom. To avoid burning out, though, you need to slow down your pace. Take time to genuinely appreciate your subordinates, and learn to share with them any credit for work well done. You'll win their gratitude and gain even more of the adulation that fuels you.

Your Finances

Dragons are driven by a desire for wealth, and the prestige, rank, and splendor that comes with it. You can become downright ruthless in your pursuit of money, and you may find yourself doing things you later regret unless you realize that wealth isn't everything. Dragons truly need to reevaluate money as their ruling god.

Health and Fitness

Given the emphasis our culture places on fitness and physical beauty, you're probably already in close to perfect shape. You like nothing more than drawing admiring stares as you strut down a beach in your bathing suit. You're a natural showoff, and sports like snowboarding and sailing are showcases for your athletic skills. But you should also try sports like swimming and biking that emphasize endurance and that will help to quiet the competitive fires that rage within you. You can also expend the energy of those fires with a healthy dose of competitive sports like tennis or racquetball. (Stay away from golf, though—it requires so much patience that as a fiery Dragon, you're likely to throw your clubs in frustration.) A Dragon's natural impatience can become a problem when it comes to diet, too. Instead of talking on the phone or watching television, when you eat your meals, try to be in the moment. You'll realize that you can get full on smaller portions, and you'll diminish your tendency toward overeating.

How to Recognize a Dragon

The Dragon's trademark flashy wardrobe calls attention to them wherever they go. As a Dragon, you'll probably be wearing expensive jewelry or driving a flashy car, since you don't shy away from ostentatious displays of wealth.

Famous Dragons

Calista Flockhart, Courteney Cox Arquette, Robin Williams, Alicia Silverstone, John Lennon, Faye Dunaway, Dr. Ruth, Keanu Reeves, Eartha Kitt

Snake

Many of your personality traits recall your legendary role in the biblical story of the Garden of Eden. You pride yourself on your wisdom and knowledge, but you can also be devious and manipulative at times. You tend to look at every situation from a controlling point of view—What can I get out of it? You make decisions quickly and firmly, yet you're also guilty of a tendency to exaggerate. When you think you're not going to get caught, you have an enormous capacity for stretching the truth. You've grown to crave the spotlight, and you despise being ignored. You were born charming and popular: people have been flocking to your side all your life. Your tremendous gift for knowledge keeps you at least one step ahead of the crowd.

Strengths

Intellectual, artistic, philosophical, sophisticated, shrewd, and sexy

Weaknesses

Deceitful, arrogant, calculating, and ruthless

Overall Self-improvement Goal

To open your heart and learn to trust others. They're not going to deceive you the way you would them.

Your Love Life

Snakes ooze sex appeal from every pore; they're masters of the art of seduction. Because of your romantic, charming nature, you've got no shortage of lovers and admirers. But commitment is a dirty word in your vocabulary. Married snakes can have stable relationships, but good luck getting one to the altar to begin with. You're too slithery to be pinned down; you'd rather surround yourself with partners who make you feel affirmed and secure each and every day. But you panic if others ask for the same thing in return. You'll have a better shot at sustaining a deep relationship if you focus on making your romance a two-way street. Consider your partner's needs and views more than your own, and learn to trust that your partner can be faithful to you. It's your own capacity for infidelity that makes you suspicious.

Your Friendships

Emotion doesn't come easily to Snakes; you have a hard time opening up to people and sharing your heart with them. Rather than delving beneath the surface, you tend to be a fair-weather friend and have been known to slither away from a buddy in need when it wasn't convenient for you to lend a helping hand. It's important for you to learn to walk the extra mile on behalf of those you care about. Snakes need praise and appreciation—your most lasting friendships will be with those who admire you and are truthful with you in the way you need to be with them.

Your Career

Snakes love a good puzzle or a mystery to solve, and you'll thrive in occupations that tap into that skill, like research, surgery, and psychology. Because Snakes are very image conscious, you need to be in work environments where pizzazz and finesse get a lot of recognition. Try to find more value in the creative process itself, to be more focused on how a project is going instead of what the end results will bring you.

Your Finances

Your finances are in good shape because Snakes shy away from risk as part of their nature. When it comes to investments, you're too smart to wager your net worth in some get-rich-quick scheme. You always have cash on hand when you need it, but you can be a bit miserly and don't like lending to others. You have a tendency to overspend, though, in your pursuit of the glitter and glamour that money can bring, buying yourself expensive accessories and adornments. Snakes often are tempted to check their morals at the bank door, so you should try to be a bit more ethical in your pursuit and spending of money.

Health and Fitness

Your tendency toward overwork and stress can cause insomnia and heart problems; you need to remember to eat proper meals and exercise regularly. Try using a personal trainer; you like to be admired, so why not do so while you're exercising? Or join a gym with lots of mirrors. It's important for you to get that kind of reflection; otherwise, it's hard for you to find a reason to exercise. Because you see eating as an aesthetic opportunity, you're likely to eat healthfully and not overindulge. Remember to take a lot of time to enjoy the beauty of colors and textures of different foods, and not to overindulge your natural sweet tooth.

How to Recognize a Snake

Snakes are lounge lizards, clad from head to toe in the latest fashions. You're the people who make the clothing industry so successful, because you have such an incredible gift for the seduction of image.

Famous Snakes

Pierce Brosnan, Courtney Love, John Malkovich, Fiona Apple, Howard Stern, Tim Allen, Kim Basinger, Maya Angelou, Bob Dylan

Horse

Like the animal they're named for, Horses are friendly, gregarious people who like to be around others. You're born hosts and devoted friends; you're the kind of person who doesn't mind being called in the middle of the night to help a friend in crisis. In fact, you love to be needed. You have boundless energy and ambition—you enjoy being physically active and stretching your muscles. But you also possess a rebellious streak: you're hot-blooded and quick to react out of anger or impatience. Some may even call you an egotist, given your tendency to preen and hog the limelight.

Strengths
Vivacious, loyal, energetic, and enthusiastic

Weaknesses
Volatile, manipulative, anxious, and self-centered

Overall Self-improvement Goals
To combat your innate flightiness. You have a tendency to run from the slightest chance of danger or risk.

Your Love Life
Horses are true romantics who will give up everything for love. You crave the closeness of intimacy, but you may also balk if you feel pressured or cornered. Your ideal partner likes big adventure as much as you do and will let you go off on grand explorations, but can also put up with your moodiness and knows how to calm you (a cube of sugar will usually do the trick). Given your natural dreaminess, you may be accused of being

fickle, but the right person can encourage you to settle down and be faithful. Deep down, you're really looking for someone to give you all the love you crave. Just don't be so quick to run at the first sign of conflict—even the most stable relationships may occasionally hit a speed bump.

Your Friendships

You pride yourself on your friendships; you're a skilled host and a popular party guest. Your limitless enthusiasm is contagious, and people enjoy being around you to bask in its reflected glow. You especially enjoy the company of those who are as eager as you are to explore the world. You love having a good time, but you're also always there for a friend in crisis, no matter the emergency. You could be a better friend still by learning the values of simplicity and stillness—there's nothing wrong with a quiet night at home with the VCR and a big bowl of popcorn.

Your Career

Horses need to be in a work environment where they can lead the pack to greener pastures, where they can take off and run with an idea. Any kind of monotony and simple routine will drive you to despair. You're a loyal, dependable worker, and once employers recognize that, they should give you free rein to explore all your dreams and visions. You're well suited for careers that give you a measure of independence, like research, teaching, writing, and performing. You should learn, though, to value what others have to say; there's something to be said for the role of consensus in decision making, especially if you plan to get along with your colleagues.

Your Finances

You're adept with money and a good financier; you're very pragmatic and appropriately concerned about input and output. But you're also famous for losing interest in your investments and becoming overly skittish. The stock market does take its dips and dives, and for long-term gains, you have to learn to ride the wave.

Health and Fitness

Horses are naturally physically active, and they adapt easily to most sports, especially those that emphasize coordination and endurance, like gymnastics, skiing, and long-distance running. It's a basic part of your nature to express your enjoyment of life physically—you've been doing so since childhood, and it's important to keep this up throughout your life. As long as you maintain your muscles in motion, you can eat pretty much whatever you want, including the junk food you crave. But if you don't keep active, you may find yourself eating beyond your body's capacity to metabolize, and gaining weight as a result. Stay active, and you'll stay in good health.

How to Recognize a Horse

Horses are brimming with vitality; you're a model of health and fitness. Others think of you as the exemplars of the human body, like the famous Michelangelo sculpture of David. You're something of a clothes horse (pardon the pun); your palette runs to the neutral shades—browns, tans, and naturals.

Famous Horses

Cindy Crawford, John Travolta, Kevin Costner, Kirstie Alley, Sean Connery, Clint Eastwood, Barbra Streisand, Sandra Bullock, Janet Jackson, Paul McCartney

Goat

A Goat's greatest gift is creativity—you're talented artists and innovators who live to explore, challenge, and discover. Your willingness to chart new territory knows no bounds; you're unconquerable dreamers. You consider yourself cultured and elegant; you have exquisite taste, and you know it. But you also have little self-control and little patience for life's realities. Your relentless pursuit of the unconventional has left you a bit unmoored. You won't easily admit it, but you're something of a worrier.

Strengths

Imaginative, unconventional, gentle, charming, and peaceful

Weaknesses

Self-indulgent, shy, hypersensitive, reckless, and indecisive

Overall Self-improvement Goals

To become more aware of how you may be trampling upon the feelings of others. You need to learn when you've pushed other people's patience to the limit.

Your Love Life

Goats are the Casanovas of the animal world. You're gifted in the art of seduction—you're caring, romantic, sensitive lovers. But you don't have a great track record for long-term commitment, as you tend to run off in pursuit of someone else who has caught your eye. Perhaps that's because you're fundamentally insecure, ever searching for the person you believe is going to love and protect you. Your ideal partner is someone who can provide you with the security you crave, understand your need for control, and yet also enjoy along with you the heightened pleasures of spontaneity. You, in turn, need to learn that commitment can bring you security without suffocating you. Try, too, to tune in more to your partner's emotional needs. After all, there are two of you in this relationship.

Your Friendships

Given their impeccable tastes in cuisine and culture, Goats are the ideal companion for a night on the town. But since they're also notoriously unreliable, as a Goat you'll have to actively remind yourself to show up on time. You need friends who'll appreciate your creativity but who aren't scared of giving you a loving push to help you meet your commitments and complete what you've started.

Your Career

Goats don't belong in the standard business world. But you've probably already figured that out on your own: you're too artistic to fit into the constraints of a nine-to-five desk job, and you need to have work that utilizes your creative vision and insight since your true talents lie in constructing new realities and implementing new designs. You may be able to make a living through your art—painting, sculpture, photography—but you can also try interior design, architecture, gardening, or another field where you can develop your craft more lucratively. Remember that you don't have to work alone—try bringing other people into your vision with you. They may have valuable insights worth sharing.

Your Finances

Money? What's money? To a Goat, it's a useless concept, one hardly worth valuing. You're impulsive with your money; spending it and investing it recklessly. You often fall prey to gambling and high-risk investment schemes, simply for the thrill of the ride. Unless you can find a generous patron who'll support you while you pursue your artistic whims, you need to think seriously about the financial realities of modern life. Post a budget on your refrigerator door, and don't carry your credit cards (in fact, maybe you shouldn't even have any) with you. Otherwise you'll be tempted to spend what you don't have—and then some.

Health and Fitness

Goats have a delicate constitution and tend to shy away from most physical activity. You need to learn to fight your natural inertia and antipathy toward exertion. You don't have to start playing team sports, but find some exercise, no matter how unconventional, that gets your heart rate going—like swimming, dancing, even fast walking. Start slowly, and pick something with long-term potential that intrigues you so it will hold your interest. And, given your tendency to be a picky eater, you may not be getting a balanced diet. It may offend your artistic sensibilities, but keep a copy of the food pyramid on hand just to remind you to get all the nutrients you need.

How to Recognize a Goat

Given their flair for the unconventional, a Goat's wardrobe may tend toward the exotic, even downright bizarre. But since you're quite conscious of looking elegant and charming, you can also be spotted in beautifully tailored suits. The giveaway is probably the level of attention paid to your appearance—you're not the type to leave the house in grungy sweatpants.

Famous Goats
Mick Jagger, Bruce Willis, Julia Roberts, Pamela Anderson Lee, Bill Gates, Christopher Walken, Barbara Walters, Debra Winger, Robert De Niro

Monkey

Curious and mischievous, Monkeys are fun-loving, occasionally naughty characters. You treat life as a jungle gym that's been custom built expressly for you—endlessly playing and scampering about, and clearly enjoying yourself immensely. Your spirit and love of life is infectious; you're always at the center of attention at parties, ever able to shine in any social situation. The fact that you're quick-witted and clever adds to your social appeal, but those skills may tend to get you into trouble because you rarely take the time to think about the consequences of your actions. You live life in the moment—for better or worse.

Strengths
Irresistible, independent, energetic, bold, ingenious, and shrewd

Weaknesses
Evasive, emotional, and opportunistic

Overall Self-improvement Goal
To balance your boundless enthusiasm with a healthy respect for responsibility

Your Love Life
You fall in love easily and often, but you fall out of love just as quickly. Because your actions are ruled by your emotions, your

love life tends to be a string of passionate affairs that end in flames. Your ideal partners are those who can keep up with your antics—and thereby keep your interest—but who can also provide you with a modest sense of equilibrium. You'll fight it tooth and nail, but you have to learn that there's a value in commitment and even (gasp) staying home. Try not to be so flighty, to be more patient with your partner (instead of running away at the first sign of something you don't like), and to be more dedicated to making your relationships work.

Your Friendships

Monkeys are easily bored, and are not comfortable being alone. So you tend to surround yourself with people like you who want to explore every branch and swing on every rope that presents itself. But while you're enjoying these diversions, you also need to build friendships of substance—someday, you'll probably need the support of friends who really care about you. Try to open your heart and let friends in, and show them in turn that you're capable of reliable, compassionate behavior.

Your Career

Work is a dirty word in a Monkey's vocabulary. Monkeys despise the boring, the routine, the dull—for you, work needs to be something that offers you variety, innovation, and even entertainment. You're full of ideas—many of them are probably half-baked and somewhat flawed—but you need to be in an atmosphere that welcomes and encourages your unique brand of creativity. You'd make an excellent entertainer, comedian, or writer—provided you learn to think before you act. You have a tendency to be reckless and make decisions on impulse. You also need to learn not to let success go to your head. A little maturity and thoughtfulness can go a long way in your career.

Your Finances

You like to "monkey" (pardon the pun—we couldn't resist) around in the stock market and enjoy the thrill of high-risk investments. Though you can be unusually ingenious with money-making ideas and hot stocks, you also need to keep your taste for risk taking in check. You may be inclined to gamble it all away at the expense of a stable income and portfolio. The occasional questionable venture may bring great rewards, but be sure not to deplete your reserves along the way.

Health and Fitness

Monkeys have tons of energy, so you're likely to be in good physical shape, easily able to burn off the calories from your constant snacking. Be sure to keep your metabolism at that high level with regular exercise or sports that involves your joy of athleticism, no matter how busy you get. Also try to keep your unquenchable taste for danger in check: you were probably the first to try out the latest "extreme" sport, but be sure to practice some restraint and wear safety equipment.

How to Recognize a Monkey

Just look for the feather boa or outrageous tie. Monkeys are the bon vivants of fashion, clad in colorful, bright, attention-grabbing clothes. In fact, we could all learn from you how to work a little more color into our wardrobes.

Famous Monkeys

Will Smith, Jennifer Aniston, Tom Hanks, Gillian Anderson, Chelsea Clinton, Danny DeVito, Andy Garcia, Dana Delaney, Tom Selleck, Elizabeth Taylor

Rooster

In your own way, you define yourself by your fanatical attention to your responsibilities, be it getting up at dawn to crow or something slightly less bucolic. You never put off for tomorrow what you can do today—you'd see doing that as a personal failing. You're therefore a bit old-fashioned, but also a reliable, trustworthy person, even if somewhat conservative at heart. You like to be noticed and to be thought of as attractive, so you tend to preen and strut about. Flattery will get a person everywhere with you. Be warned that some people may be turned off by your vanity and tendency to constantly check your appearance in any reflective surface you happen to pass.

Strengths
Honest, industrious, flamboyant, and straightforward

Weaknesses
Arrogant, pompous, fanatical, and scattered

Overall Self-improvement Goals
To keep your sense of self-importance in check

Your Love Life
As a Rooster, you're a flirt who actively seeks out the attentions of the opposite sex. You don't settle down and enter a relationship easily, and you'll play a bit hard-to-get along the way. Your ideal partner is someone who can be patient with you and your need for flattery; a person who is quietly powerful enough to calm your anxieties. In turn, you should try to give more back to your partner, to learn the value of someone else's insight. Feel

free to share your opinions about the "right" way of doing things—but remember to ask what your partner may think, too.

Your Friendships

You're a devoted friend who keeps your promises, and you don't make them lightly. By the same token, when others don't live up to your standards or expectations, you're often devastated. Try to widen your social network to people who aren't all necessarily replicas of you, people who can open up your mind to new ways of thinking, even if you disagree with them.

Your Career

Roosters are hardworking and loyal, an asset to any office. Whatever the job, you'll get it done—and given your ambition, you'll be doing so with an eye toward moving up the ladder. You should seek out professions that can give you that sense of prestige and status that's so important to you, while also bringing out your penchant for artistry and flamboyance. You'd be an ideal movie producer, actor, or musician; you might also try troubleshooting fields like detective work, medicine, psychiatry, or engineering. Explore new ways of doing things, instead of clinging to the old tried-and-true.

Your Finances

Because you're obsessed with appearances and style, you have a tendency to spend too much money far too quickly on the latest fashions (as long as they're tasteful, of course). You're a bit too impulsive when it comes to spending what you earn, so seek out the advice of someone who can help keep an eye on your finances. A software program can also help keep a running tab on your savings to make sure you continue to live within your means.

Health and Fitness

The thought of being out of shape or unattractive terrifies you and keeps you going to the gym on a regular basis. Try to have fun with it, though, and enjoy yourself. You don't have to do the same thing every day. Think of exercise as a buffet, with plenty of varieties available. Sign up for a karate class, join a volleyball league, go biking in the park. You're a bit of a traditionalist, too, when it comes to food—try to push yourself to try new tastes and cuisines.

How to Recognize a Rooster

Roosters are fashion conscious to their core. You gravitate, though, toward the labels that are conservative, discreet, and refined like Calvin Klein or Ralph Lauren. You're too much of a traditionalist to risk a Versace fashion statement.

Famous Roosters

Michelle Pfeiffer, Melanie Griffith, Deborah Harry, Steve Martin, Dolly Parton, Gloria Estefan, Eric Clapton, Larry King, Bette Midler, Goldie Hawn, Carol Burnett, Michael Caine, Katharine Hepburn

Dog

Like the animal they're named for, Dogs are loyal, trustworthy friends. Time and again, you'll put the needs of others ahead of your own, because you truly enjoy helping others in any way you can. You're guided by your profound sense of duty and righteousness; you'll fight tirelessly for the underdog, the oppressed, or whatever worthy cause has caught your attention. You were seemingly born old, and you take everything very seriously, which makes you a bit watchful and worrisome. When panic strikes, you can turn nasty out of a sense of self-preservation and protectionism of those you love.

Strengths
Persevering, courageous, gregarious, faithful, moral, intelligent, and forgiving

Weaknesses
Stubborn, sarcastic, proud, judgmental, worrisome, and neurotic

Overall Self-improvement Goals
To imbue life with a greater sense of wonder instead of fear

Your Love Life
As a Dog, you're a romantic in that you believe in true love; you're looking for a soul mate who'll provide you the constant reassurance you crave. Dogs will always have problems romantically because of the eternal anxiety they feel; it takes you a long time to trust others because people can easily take advantage of your boundless affection. Dogs need a partner who will provide all the affection they desire, offering a mix of dependability and passion. Although you like to follow, as a Dog you don't like to be commanded by people who don't have integrity or who aren't compassionate. A good romantic goal for Dogs is to try to let go of your anxieties and enjoy the roller-coaster nature of romance. It can be somewhat scary, but you'll reap greater rewards.

Your Friendships
Dogs like to feel like they're part of a pack, so you actively seek out social situations where you're in a group. Others are drawn

to you for your social nature; you mix in easily and rarely rock the boat. You're a good listener, and you're quick to offer friends a shoulder to cry on. Be careful, though, in choosing your friends. Because of your giving nature, you're prone to being taken advantage of, especially after you have given so much of yourself and made costly sacrifices for others. Your best friends are those people like you who are constant and welcoming yet who enjoy the occasional good chase or adventure.

Your Career

As a Dog, you're a valuable asset wherever you work, because you commit yourself to your duties with every ounce of your energy. You're often the first one in to the office, and the last one to go home. Because you're able to see a situation clearly from all sides, you'd thrive in a profession that utilizes your intelligence and compassion, such as a lawyer, judge, social worker, or educator. You're happiest in work that has a real mission to it so you can experience a long-term sense of service and accomplishment. Be sure, though, to ease up on the zeal of your mission in order to listen from all points of view. You need to take time off and learn to relax: otherwise your health will suffer for it.

Your Finances

Since you've probably been working since the age of ten, you know the value of a dollar and have a solid financial picture. Dogs can be quite intractable about saving and earning money, and they don't take risks lightly. But this can make you get in your own way, if you become too thrifty and frightened of losing resources. Some risks may be worth taking, so solicit the opinion of a trusted advisor.

Health and Fitness

Anyone who's ever had a dog as a pet knows that it will eat whatever is in front of it. It's likely that you're guilty of the same bad habit. You're a great dinner guest because you love to eat, and others revel in your obvious enjoyment of food. But you should try to cultivate a more refined palate, and restrain yourself from snacking all day long. Exercise is critical to your health because you have a propensity for stress-related illnesses, and regular physical exercise can help alleviate the stress that can can make you ill. You're not a team-sport person—you prefer cooperation to competitiveness—but you might find bicycling, walking, or swimming to be activities that you'll enjoy and that will keep you in top shape.

How to Recognize a Dog

Dogs have a warm, welcoming sense of style. You wouldn't want to dress in a way that might be misconstrued as threatening; what you wear and how you carry yourself conveys your approachable, cheerful nature. The colors of most of your clothes are earth tones; your home is filled with a clutter of personal touches, especially photographs of friends and family members.

Famous Dogs

Sharon Stone, Madonna, Jamie Lee Curtis, Andre Agassi, Mariah Carey, Claudia Schiffer, Prince, Connie Chung, Prince William, Candice Bergen, Michael Jackson

Pig

Pigs live according to the pleasure principle. You have an insatiable appetite for life and you strive to enjoy all its gifts to the fullest, which makes you a gregarious, generous person. All the other "animals" enjoy your company immensely, because you so openly welcome them, despite their flaws. Yet you can be lazy and self-indulgent, and at times, something of a snob.

Strengths

Cultured, sensual, brave, strong, scintillating, and chivalrous

Weaknesses

Materialistic, lustful, reckless, and torporous

Overall Self-improvement Goals

To learn to enjoy simplicity as much as you enjoy the gourmet life

Your Love Life

Pigs want to be swept off their feet into a passionate romance, and have no trouble making a long-term commitment. But you're also possessive, jealous, and exclusive, and the slightest sign of a hitch in the romance sends you reeling. You should seek out partners who will indulge you in the size and proportion of epic romance, but you must also learn how to cultivate the art of quiet contemplative love.

Your Friendships

You're a good companion and have many friends. You especially seek out those who can provide you with avenues for knowledge of and exposure to the arts and culture you enjoy so much. But you tend to be overly sensitive. Learn to wait and give others the benefit of the doubt. They may not have meant to hurt you.

Your Career

When it comes to work, Pigs have great ideas and the sky's the limit, but they need to scale down their visions to meet the natural restraints of the physical world, not to mention their innate laziness and dislike of hard labor. As a Pig, you're well suited for the movie business or restaurant and hotel management—anything where you're free to have dreams of expansion while someone else is there to figure out the details and handle the work. You'd also enjoy service-oriented careers where you could work to help others, as a teacher, counselor, or veterinarian. All in all, though, work isn't that important to you; you're not as ambitious as some of the other animals. You'd rather enjoy life than spend it at the office.

Your Finances

Money only interests Pigs as a means of satisfying their tastes for the finer things in life. So though you're not particularly ambitious, you recognize your own need for an opulent lifestyle, and usually find some means of earning to meet those demands. Try not to be too piggy when it comes to money, though, and remember to give to charity, as well as keep your expenses in check. The best things in life aren't necessarily the most expensive.

Health and Fitness

The problem is not that Pigs are gluttons but that they enjoy food so immensely, especially good food. When you overeat—as you are wont to do—you do so in the finest restaurants. You'd be miserable if you cut yourself off from fine dining completely, so instead you need to learn a bit of balance. Try planning your menus ahead of time, because you tend to eat without a sense of tomorrow. If you actually plot out your meals, you're more likely to eat in moderation and nutritiously. You should also plan out a regular routine of exercise, especially aerobic activity that can help you trim down and mitigate any weight gain from your culinary exploits.

How to Recognize a Pig

Pigs are regal dressers, not shy of ostentatious displays of wealth and style. You dress in deep, rich colors—indigo, dark blue, rich red—and gravitate toward luxurious fabrics like velvet.

Famous Pigs

Winona Ryder, Val Kilmer, Minnie Driver, Billy Crystal, Jada Pinkett Smith, Stephen King, Noah Wyle, Emma Thompson, Woody Allen, Hillary Rodham Clinton, Farrah Fawcett, Steven Spielberg, Elton John

Best and Worst Matches

SIGN	COMPATIBLE	LESS COMPATIBLE
Rat	Rabbit, Dragon, Monkey	Horse, Snake, Pig
Ox	Rooster, Snake, Tiger	Goat, Dragon
Tiger	Horse, Dog, Monkey	Rabbit, Pig
Rabbit	Rat, Ox, Snake	Tiger, Rooster, Dog, Dragon
Dragon	Rat, Tiger, Snake, Horse	Ox, Rabbit, Dog
Snake	Rabbit, Dragon, Rooster	Snake, Dog, Pig
Horse	Dragon, Horse, Rooster, Dog	Rat, Rabbit, Monkey
Goat	Pig, Monkey, Dog	Ox, Goat, Rooster
Monkey	Rat, Tiger, Goat	Snake, Horse, Monkey
Rooster	Ox, Snake, Horse	Rooster, Rabbit, Goat
Dog	Horse, Monkey, Dog	Rabbit, Dragon, Snake
Pig	Goat, Monkey, Rooster, Ox	Snake, Pig, Rabbit

Best and Worst Friends

SIGN	COMPATIBLE	LESS COMPATIBLE
Rat	Ox, Rabbit, Dragon, Monkey	Horse, Goat, Rooster
Ox	Rat, Rabbit, Snake, Rooster	Tiger, Goat
Tiger	Horse, Goat, Dog	Ox, Tiger, Snake
Rabbit	Rat, Ox, Snake, Goat, Pig	Horse, Monkey, Rooster
Dragon	Rat, Snake, Monkey, Pig	Ox, Goat, Dog
Snake	Tiger, Monkey	Rabbit, Dragon
Horse	Tiger, Goat, Pig	Rat, Rabbit, Monkey
Goat	Rabbit, Horse, Pig	Rat, Rooster, Dragon
Monkey	Rat, Dragon, Pig	Tiger, Rabbit, Snake
Rooster	Ox, Snake	Rabbit, Goat, Rooster
Dog	Tiger, Horse, Pig	Dragon
Pig	Dragon, Monkey, Dog	Tiger, Snake, Pig

Best and Worst Colleagues

SIGN	COMPATIBLE	LESS COMPATIBLE
Rat	Dragon, Ox, Monkey	Rat, Tiger, Horse
Ox	Rat, Snake, Horse	Dragon, Rooster, Dog
Tiger	Horse, Rabbit, Dog	Tiger, Monkey, Pig
Rabbit	Goat, Pig, Rabbit, Snake	Dragon, Dog, Pig
Dragon	Rat, Snake	Tiger, Rabbit, Rooster
Snake	Rabbit, Dragon, Rooster	Horse, Monkey, Pig
Horse	Ox, Dog, Pig	Rat, Snake, Monkey
Goat	Rabbit, Dog, Pig	Tiger, Dragon, Rooster
Monkey	Rat, Dog, Pig	Tiger, Snake, Monkey
Rooster	Rat, Snake, Monkey	Ox, Dragon, Rooster
Dog	Rat, Monkey	Ox, Rooster, Rabbit
Pig	Monkey, Rooster	Tiger, Snake, Dog

7

Numerology

*H*ave we got *your* number! Not only is it possible to gain predictive insights into your future through numerology, but this ancient art can also reveal deep-seated truths about your personality. By identifying your "life path" number, you can acquire a powerful tool for introspection and self-revelation. Numerology can help you understand more about yourself physically, emotionally, and spiritually.

Like many of the other methods in this book, numerology dates back thousands of years. Some people credit Pythagoras as the first to look at numbers in order to divine the future—some 2,500 years ago—but we also know that numerology was used by the ancient Hindus and Chinese as a way to find insights into the meaning of life.

According to the principles of numerology, all life is governed by the numbers one to nine. Each of us has been assigned one of these numbers at birth, determined by the digits in our date of birth. Your number contains both positive and negative qualities that influence you and your life experiences. The more you know about your numerological strengths and weaknesses, the better equipped you will be to make the most of your personal potential.

You'll never look at numbers the same way again!

What Number Are You?

Your "life path" number represents the traits that will carry you through life. Determining your life path number is a simple calculation using the month, day, and year of your birth.

In numerology, all numbers, no matter how large, can be added up to form a single digit between one and nine. To find your life path number, simply add up the numbers of your month, day, and year (include all four digits). If you end up with a double-digit number, simply add the two digits together to get a single digit. For example, if your date of birth is December 31, 1970 (Debra's), your life path number is $1+2+3+1+1+9+7+0=24$. Then $2+4=6$, so your life path number is 6. Jennifer's birthday is January 29, 1958, so her life path number is $1+2+9+1+9+5+8=35$; $3+5=8$. Got it?

Ones

Ones are the numerological leaders—the high-attaining, high-achieving trailblazers of the worlds they live and work in. Ones believe unfailingly in the strengths of their own convictions, which often brings them tremendous success and accomplishment. As a One, your boundless confidence is seductive to all those around you, but your self-assurance comes at a price. Critics might call you self-centered, and you tend to alienate people around you, because you insist on having your own way *all the time*. Your unquenchable ambition also makes you restless, always searching for the next project or striving to climb the next rung of the ladder.

Strengths

Highly individual, strong sense of self, immensely capable, and driven

Weaknesses

Domineering, impatient, willful, quick-tempered, and aloof

Overall Self-improvement Goals

To become more compassionate and open to the needs of others without losing your own sense of direction. Independence doesn't have to mean isolation. You can bring people close to you without feeling that you're leaning on them.

Romance

Ones tend to be status conscious and concerned with appearances, so in addition to seeking a mate who is dependable and faithful, if truth be told, you'd be happiest with an attractive person who looks good in your company. You need to remind yourself to look beneath the surface, though, since no One will be satisfied for long with someone who's simply a piece of arm candy. Try to share more of yourself; by opening yourself up to even a hint of vulnerability, you may find that you can learn a thing or two from your partner (though you may think you have nothing to learn from anyone!). Ones tend to have a Teflon coating of self-sufficiency, so you may find that the determined, if not drop-dead gorgeous, neighbor down the hall will be the one who can stick with his pursuit, penetrate your shell, and ultimately win your heart.

Friendship

As a One, you tend to seek friends who reflect your own status—powerful, influential people who can help you get what you want. But since friendship is a two-way street, you need to remember to be more sensitive and aware of your friends' needs. Don't forget to ask what *you* can do for them every so often.

Work

Ones want to be at the top. If you're not already there, you're well on your way, and you won't rest until you finish your journey. Ones have the vision, the determination, and they want the rewards. But you should let others help you as you climb the ladder—and especially once you get there, if you intend to stick around. In order to bring more reciprocity and equality into your decision making, consider polling your colleagues for opinions other than your own. Learn to praise as much as you criticize. As long as you're in control, you'll do well as a CEO of any business or private enterprise.

Money

Ones usually have a huge bankroll and portfolio commensurate with their level of success. But you tend to get too caught up in the attainment of money at the expense of all else. Money is a poor substitute for human connection and fulfillment. Remind yourself that a full wallet may warm your pocket, but it can't warm your heart. Make it a goal to give a certain monthly percentage of your income to charity.

Health and Fitness

Since fitness is king (or queen, for that matter) of our culture today, the body of the ultracompetitive One is probably in top shape—and you show it off at every opportunity. But your regimen of exercise and nutrition is probably too rigid, so consider adding some balance. Relax a bit and add some contemplative time to your workout. Row on a quiet lake; take a hike in the mountains; go for a long walk; sign up for a Pilates or relaxation class. You'll stretch your muscles as well as your imagination. Focus on slowing down when you eat, too. You tend to be so preoccupied with getting things done that you may not even notice what you're eating. Look at your food, smell it, really taste it. Trust us—you'll enjoy it.

How to Recognize a One

Ones are always dressed for success. Your clearly expensive clothing screams power and demands attention. When you walk into a room, heads turn as people feel the impact of your presence. And you love every minute of it.

Famous Ones

George Clooney, Sean Connery, Daniel Day-Lewis, Elizabeth Hurley, Kevin Kline, David Letterman, Jack Nicholson, Kate Winslet, Tom Hanks

Twos

Twos are the King Solomons of numerology—masters of compromise, ideal negotiators and peacemakers. As a Two, you're probably a friend to everyone, and everyone is proud to call you his or her friend. Twos value peace and harmony above all, and strive to attain balance in all areas of life. You can, however, bend over backward to maintain the peace, even if doing so is ultimately self-destructive or alienates others. Your self-confidence may tend to suffer when you can't fix a problem, so you tend to slip easily into shyness and timidity.

Strengths
Responsive, sensitive, romantic, sympathetic, and honest

Weaknesses
Envious, passive, lethargic, apathetic, pessimistic, and unambitious

Overall Self-improvement Goals
To enjoy the benefits of being valued for your faithfulness, but to challenge yourself to stick up for yourself now and then, instead of putting others' needs ahead of your own.

Romance
You're a romantic at heart, a lover of candlelit dinners and long walks on the beach. Twos seem to be perpetually in search of the perfect soul mate, the fairy tale romance. You're very comfortable taking a position on the sidelines, and so you enjoy being with someone who's the center of attention, a dynamic, opinionated person who takes life by the horns. But don't let your partner overshadow you. Focus on becoming more assertive about your own needs, and more direct about your personal preferences. Sometimes you should get to pick the restaurant or the movie!

Friendship
Twos are extremely sensitive, and they expect their friends to be the same. Your best buddies are those who are emotional and

kind, but also truthful. Since you tend to bottle up your feelings of anger and hurt when others disappoint you, you need to form relationships with people with whom you can feel comfortable being completely honest. Work on sharing your hurts and disappointments. Your friends are probably unaware that they've even wounded you at all.

Work

The Two's skills as a negotiator and mediator are highly prized at work; you're often the best person behind whoever's in charge. You thrive in a position where you can augment the organization you work for and/or its leaders. Though you don't want the glory for yourself, you bask in its reflected glow as vice president, chief of staff, number two, even administrative assistant. You can be an even better right hand to your boss if you set clear limits on what you will and won't do. Don't let your supervisor's identity completely eclipse your own.

Money

Security is one of the Two's biggest concerns, so you tend to be careful and considered about your spending habits. You're like a squirrel, stealthily putting away pennies, slowly building a nest egg. You prefer the slow and steady road to one paved with risks, but this means you're not ever likely to make huge investments and reap huge profits. While there's nothing wrong with this philosophy, you may want to take a small considered risk from time to time, say, investing in a small high-tech stock with solid potential. In general, though, remember to stick to the courage of your convictions, and avoid pushy brokers who encourage you to throw caution to the wind.

Health and Fitness

Twos often equate food with love, which means you may tend to overeat. Focus on challenging your self-indulgent appetite with commonsense exercise and nutrition habits. You're a classic yo-yo dieter; you can easily get into a pattern of starving, then gorging, then starving yourself again. Resist the urge to try the latest fad diet; just make sensible adjustments to your eating habits. The same goes for exercise. You're the type who'll start training for a marathon on a whim, then spend the next few months on the couch, berating yourself for having failed. You do need to have a dynamic program of exercise, so talk to a personal trainer about a combination of aerobics and weight lifting to keep your metabolism active.

How to Recognize a Two

Twos tend to be seductive in a warm, nurturing way. You usually wear soft, comfortable fabrics; your voice is soothing and inviting.

Famous Twos

Jennifer Aniston, Pierce Brosnan, John Cusack, Billy Crystal, Robert Downey, Jr., William Hurt, Michael Jordan, Michelle Pfeiffer, Kim Basinger, Kenneth Branagh

Threes

Threes are party animals, social butterflies who revel in going out and being seen. You love to entertain and be entertained, and thrill in being the center of attention. Threes are also very creative and enjoy sharing their talents with the world—as writers, speakers, or actors, perhaps. Your energy effervesces and ignites a room as you enter, but being an Energizer bunny is also your fatal flaw. You're so full of energy that you expend it too freely and sometimes wastefully.

Strengths

Engaging, magnetic, expressive, creative, warm, and outgoing

Weaknesses

Scattered, self-serving, frivolous, superficial, vain, impatient, and intolerant

Overall Self-improvement Goals

To become more moderate and thoughtful in your relentless search for more: more fun, more power, more thrills

Romance

Threes are always looking for someone to provide the attention they crave, someone who'll laugh at their jokes and keep them amused and stimulated. As a Three, your worst fear is boredom in a relationship; you're not the type to enjoy sitting home and popping an old movie in the VCR. Your tendency to chatter and prattle and fill silences can be a turnoff to some, so to find the partner of your dreams, work on being more thoughtful, deep, and sincere with those you love. Others will appreciate the effort, which can only strengthen your relationships.

Friendship

Your happy-go-lucky attitude makes you popular. You're usually surrounded by quick-witted, adoring peers. But you need to learn to share the limelight from time to time. Remember to slow down and shine a little attention on those around you. Ask if there's anything you can do for them—and follow through with whatever they ask of you.

Work

You'd absolutely suffocate if forced to slave away in a traditional office setting. You need to be in a versatile, creative field like advertising, landscaping, crafts, the arts. Even though you don't mind the risks of entrepreneurship, you'd be well served to be more cautious in your pursuits, and more inclusive of those around you. Threes tend to think they're the belles of the ball, and might be in for trouble if they start their own business without realizing that they're not the only ones with enviable talents.

Money

Blessed (or cursed, perhaps) with a general lack of concern about tomorrow, you're a charter member of the make-it-so-I-can-spend-it school of financial management. Spending money may be one of your skills, but handling it isn't. You need to learn the value of a penny saved—at the very least, it keeps the creditors at bay. Ask for help from a financial advisor in establishing a monthly budget and savings schedule. Then you can play as much as you want, and still have enough left over for a rainy day.

Health and Fitness

Since you tend to bring your extremist attitude to health and fitness, you'll swim fifty miles one day, and then you won't exercise for months. You need to establish a routine of diet and exercise with a time limit (say, one set of tennis) so won't be tempted to obsessively spend hours at it. A same-day, same-time workout may seem humdrum to you, but it will work wonders for your physical and mental health. And bring that same approach to your diet, making sure you eat three balanced meals a day instead of depriving yourself.

How to Recognize a Three

Look in the center of the room—that's where the Three will be holding court. Then again, it shouldn't be hard to spot you: you've got a love/love relationship with bold, bright colors.

Famous Threes

Alec Baldwin, Ellen Barkin, Cameron Diaz, Jenna Elfman, Jodie Foster, Jennifer Lopez, Andie MacDowell, Brad Pitt, Winona Ryder, Sting, Barbara Walters, Brendan Fraser

Fours are the human equivalent of a security blanket. You're internally well grounded, and you have a grounding effect on others. A pillar of the community, you're trusted by all who know you. You're valued for your common sense and practicality, and others often turn to you to plan and organize anything, since you'll do so flawlessly. You tend, however, to be tenacious and set in your ways of doing things. Caught up in the routine of daily affairs, you may miss the big picture of life.

Strengths

Industrious, tenacious, sensible, courageous, and down-to-earth

Weaknesses

Depressive, obstinate, dogmatic, narrow-minded, and overly cautious

Overall Self-improvement Goals

To learn to enjoy risk taking and the steady momentum of building a future

Romance

Fours crave security and comfort above all else, and are happiest in long-term, committed relationships. You're hardly one for torrid affairs, but once you feel safe, your passionate side emerges. Your ideal partner is someone who can bring out your sensuality by offering you the safety net you crave, and also challenging you to open yourself up to new experiences. To be a better partner, try to be less controlling and more flexible in your love life. Take an occasional backseat to your mate's preferences and habits, and let spontaneity occasionally chart your course.

Friendship

Fours usually have few friends, but they are all very close, and once made, these friendships will last a lifetime. You seek out people who are steady and patient but who can be lighthearted in the face of your stubbornness. You can be a better friend to them if you let yourself go a little. Demand less, and enjoy more.

Work

Fours are the trusted workers of any office, the ones who work tirelessly around the clock to get the job done. You're well suited for positions that require steadfastness and loyalty; you'll take a boss's secrets to the grave. While you'd be an invaluable employee in any job, service-oriented careers like nursing or teaching play especially well to your strengths. In the long run, it will benefit you to take chances sometimes. Make yourself go for the big promotion or ask for a raise instead of resenting other people when they get the brass ring you've been quietly eyeing.

Money

To be perfectly blunt, you're a tightwad. When you open your wallet, moths fly out. When a group of friends go out to dinner, you're the one who whips out the calculator to figure out each person's contribution to the penny, including tip. Before everyone starts calling you Scrooge behind your back (if they don't do so already!), try to loosen your hold on your earnings. Fight your urge toward miserliness with occasional splurges on something frivolous or luxurious that you've had your eye on, or with a donation to a worthy charity.

Health and Fitness

Fours tend to be a bit sedentary, stuck in the exercise routine they learned in high school. The rules have changed since then, and it would be good for you to open yourself up to new experiences. Try kick boxing or Pilates or yoga class or whatever's the current craze at your gym. Your exercise routine could probably use a blast of diversity and a change of atmosphere, as could your diet. Don't be afraid of trying new cuisines or experimenting with new trends. You're not the type to overindulge, so relax and treat yourself once in a while.

How to Recognize a Four

Fours dress in warm, comforting earth tones, from their sensible shoes to their no-nonsense hairstyle (which is probably the same one they had in high school!). Fours are unfailingly loyal to their basic fashions.

Famous Fours

Woody Allen, Bono, Russell Crowe, Rupert Everett, Helen Hunt, Nicole Kidman, Regis Philbin, Tim Robbins, Quentin Tarantino

Fives

Look to the top of a mountain, and you'll probably see a Five leading a climb up the treacherous slope. You're a die-hard adventurer and explorer. Always on the move, you have a deep-seated need to discover and experience the world. But while your free spirit may have led you around the globe, it's also kept you from facing reality. Some accuse you of lacking direction as you go on your restless search for the next big challenge. Driven by a need for change and a fear of routine, you're a jack of all trades but master of none.

Strengths

Versatile, clever, original, resourceful, and curious

Weaknesses

Hedonistic, reckless, irresponsible, self-indulgent, and unreliable

Overall Self-improvement Goals

To slow down and learn to enjoy the moment. Take your foot off the gas pedal, and notice all the important things that you've been whizzing by at top speed.

Romance

Fives are easily seduced by flashiness and excitement; that's what attracts you to others. But given your passion for change, you tend to have a problem with commitment. It's important for you to recognize that while change is vital to any relationship, there's also value in constancy. Try to be more considerate and trustworthy, and above all, patient, especially in moments that may seem dull. Life—and love—are in the details.

Friendship

Since your restless energy is contagious, you make friends easily. You surround yourself with traveling companions who can keep up with you; you run from those who seem too serious or demanding. Try to slow down every once in a while, and take stock in the people standing by your side. You may not realize how much an occasional moment of sentiment or nostalgia can deepen your friendship.

Work

Fives abhor anything routine or humdrum; you'd never be found behind a desk, in a cubicle, punching a clock at a nine-to-five job. You need challenging, thought-provoking work, and you're constantly trying new do-it-yourself, get-rich-quick schemes. There's nothing wrong with going into business for yourself—forging your own path and pursuing your own dreams—but you tend to be a bit irresponsible about the reality of business. Hire a fiscally-minded, detail-oriented partner who'll keep an eye on the books for you.

Money

You love taking risks, no matter the impact on your net worth. While you tend to make money easily, you'll quickly squander every cent on an investment that piques your interest. As a result, your financial situation tends to fluctuate widely. To get a better grip on your financial future, continue taking risks (since they often pay off for you), but be sure to set aside something secure. Maintain an untouchable nest egg so you'll have money in the bank, just in case your hallmark luck runs out.

Health and Fitness

High-strung Fives should stay away from frenetic, aggressive activities like kick boxing or spinning. Instead, try something meditative like yoga or Pilates. You should do some sort of exercise that's (gasp) mundane and routine so that you can learn to appreciate the value of discipline. Make sure you stay away from addictive foods like nicotine, caffeine, and sugar, which will only speed up your already revving metabolism. Protein and root vegetables will ground you, so that you can focus your considerable energies on the present.

How to Recognize a Five

Fives are trendsetters, unafraid to take fashion risks. You enjoy exploring the style world as eagerly as you explore the physical world.

Famous Fives

Andre Agassi, Michael J. Fox, Bette Midler, Dennis Miller, Willie Nelson, Dennis Quaid, Carly Simon, Uma Thurman, Denzel Washington

Sixes

Sixes are lovers, nurturers, protectors. You're the shoulder everyone cries on, the rock that supports others through every crisis. You have a strong, abiding sense of responsibility that guides your life, but often at the expense of your own identity.

Sixes don't feel truly happy unless someone else needs them. You carry more than your fair share of emotional burdens (your own and others'), but you do so with a smile. The question is, are you gritting your teeth behind that grin?

Strengths

Loving, compassionate, understanding, and generous

Weaknesses

Lazy, gossipy, easily overwhelmed, self-critical, and apprehensive

Overall Self-improvement Goals

To value your own needs and let go of your fears

Romance

Highly romantic Sixes are incredibly giving and affectionate, and they want to be with someone who appreciates their limitless capacity for love. But to build a strong partnership, you need to learn to give love without expecting it in return. You also need to be more assertive and honest with yourself and your partner about your own wants and needs in the relationship.

Friendship

Along with home and family, friendship is one of the most important aspects of your life. You like to surround yourself with a large and diverse selection of creative, easygoing, humorous friends. It's important for you to appreciate quality as well as quantity, so try to develop and cherish each friendship individually. Be more consistent with your displays of affection, and take your share of responsibility for any conflict instead of swallowing your feelings and not standing up for yourself.

Work

Sixes thrive in an environment that requires patience, affection, diligence, and cheerleading. You're always ready to offer advice and service, and so you belong in a helping profession, like that of a therapist, nurse, doctor, or guidance counselor. You are good at providing leadership by example, so don't be afraid to state your opinions clearly and forthrightly, even if you don't think it's what someone else wants to hear. Even though you don't like to address conflict, remind yourself that it's okay if everyone doesn't always get along. Though you often feel that helping others is its own reward, you should allow yourself to be praised for what you do. You deserve it.

Money

Sixes aren't materialists, but they're also not very good savers. You're too busy trying to keep the peace to worry about your own pocketbook. You need to be more savvy when it comes to savings, retirement, and health care, and to enlist the help of others in organizing and maintaining your finances.

Health and Fitness

Sixes tend to have an ethereal approach to life, which carries over to their bodies. Unfortunately, if you don't take your personal health more seriously, you may develop problems that will really force you to take better care of your self. Before that happens, pay attention to the nutritional value of food, not just the aesthetics of food preparation and presentation. Concentrate on exercise that's inspiring as well as motivational—perhaps dance set to music. Meditation can be a good tool for centering yourself and withstanding the high levels of emotional stress, fatigue, and exhaustion you probably suffer.

How to Recognize a Six

You're warm, welcoming, and approachable; you almost always have your arm around someone. People feel an instinctive need to run up to you and hug you. And nothing could make you happier!

Famous Sixes

Matthew Broderick, Claire Danes, Sarah Michelle Gellar, Michael Jackson, Heather Locklear, Rosie O'Donnell, Steven Spielberg, Meryl Streep, Bruce Willis

Sevens

You're an observer, but a thoughtful, analytical one. You enjoy sitting on the sidelines because it affords you the opportunity to learn about others. Given the choice, you'd rather be home with a good book than schmoozing at a crowded cocktail party. You crave quiet time for yourself, but too much solitude can make you feel lonely and unapproachable.

Strengths

Analytical, intuitive, introspective, knowledgeable, and intellectual

Weaknesses

Aloof, reserved, selfish, secretive, and pessimistic

Overall Self-improvement Goals

To blend your philosophical, analytical nature with open-minded, openhearted compassion for yourself and others. Push yourself more to go out in the world, to try new experiences and bring others into your life.

Romance

Because of your incredibly deep sensitivity, you're a wonderful lover. Your ideal partner is someone who is patient, thoughtful, and willing to listen for hours on end to your brilliant (and not-so-brilliant) ideas. But you have a vulnerable heart, and you sometimes put on airs to protect yourself and build walls between you and your lover by pretending you don't care. Open up to those you care about; you won't find true love otherwise. While you enjoy being heard, try to become a better listener yourself, to give as much as you demand from those you love.

Friendship

Because you prefer being alone, you probably don't have a wide circle of friends. But you do have a core group of two or three who are soul mates for life. Your best friends are intellectuals like you, people who stimulate your mind with thought-provoking conversation. But you need to learn to share with your heart as well as your mind. Try to be more sympathetic and sensitive to the emotional needs of others. Make an effort to be more social, to join office activities and conservation. And remember to be warm and to smile, because your characteristic reserve can often be mistaken for snobbery.

Work

Sevens are the absentminded professors, the scientists, the inventors, the philosophers. You need complete autonomy in your work and the space to invent, dream, and imagine. Though Sevens can be brilliant idea generators, you can be more successful at work by understanding the needs of others, no matter how

187

mundane they may seem to you. Learn to trust that your ideals just might be improved by other people's input, and your colleagues may be able to give you a new perspective on a problem you've been struggling with. Instead of isolating yourself in your cubicle, put aside your skepticism, and yes, *talk* to your colleagues.

Money

When it comes to money, Sevens are completely witless. You're incapable of thinking about money as a realistic concept; you hate to think of your work in terms of its material rewards. You may therefore be taken advantage of by those who are unscrupulous in business. So you'd be wise to find a trusted advisor who can monitor your financial future and to invest in a computer program to track your day-to-day spending.

Health and Fitness

With your focus and attention so heavily on your mind, you need to remember to take care of your body, too. Start by taking long walks, which give you time to think while putting your body to work. But that won't be enough—you'll eventually need to step up the pace and get your heart pumping. Try long bike rides or running, activities that you can do alone but that also provide a great aerobic benefit. Stay away from organized classes, though. The gym isn't the place for you to practice your unpolished social skills. Another good idea for Sevens is a regular massage to remind you to honor your body as well as your mind. Sevens tend to think of food as a necessary inconvenience, and usually eat whatever is handy, regardless of its nutritional content. Gourmet cooking classes may help you apply your obsession with formulas to the art of creating healthy, nutritious, tasty foods.

How to Recognize a Seven

Sevens are fashion ostriches, crying out for a makeover. Your shirt (probably a relic from the 1970s) is probably on backward; your hair is often disheveled (do you even own a hairbrush?). And you're perpetually on the verge of tripping over whatever is in front of you.

Famous Sevens

Ralph Fiennes, Carrie Fisher, Mel Gibson, Whoopi Goldberg, Al Pacino, Julia Roberts, Susan Sarandon, Jerry Seinfeld, Emma Thompson, Ethan Hawke

Eights

Driven by ambition, Eights worship at the temple of Donald Trump. You've got little time for pie-in-the-sky dreams or visions; every step you take is a well-thought-out move guiding you inexorably higher up the ladder of success. Power and status are your ultimate goals, and the quest for both informs your life, through and through. But these are goals with negative aspects, too, and in your relentless march, you'll find it very easy to neglect home and family along the way.

Strengths

Enduring, determined, ambitious, and practical

Weaknesses

Rigid, competitive, materialistic, dictatorial, and self-centered

Overall Self-improvement Goals

To free yourself from your slavery to wealth and power

Romance

Power is one of life's strongest aphrodisiacs. And because Eights have it in spades, they rarely lack for willing romantic partners. An Eight's ideal partner probably has something to offer you in terms of social status and wealth, but your relationships need to delve beneath the surface. You need to be involved with someone you can depend on and open up to. To deepen your relationships, you must be able to share your vulnerabilities with your partner. But be careful—self-centered Eights must make a real effort to be more relaxed and receptive to their partners' needs, too.

Friendship

Eights surround themselves with like-minded movers and shakers, the power brokers of the world and the circles they move in. But you need to learn to enjoy people for who they are instead of what they have. Make it a goal to prove that you can be faithful when the chips are down. Share more of your inner doubts: true friends will love and support you, whatever your inner demons or weaknesses.

Work

It's no surprise that Eights need to be the boss—you don't take instruction well. Your ideal job offers the control you need as well as the high visibility and recognition you crave. You're well suited for a career as CEO, chairman, manager, or producer. Armed with the courage of your convictions, you're well equipped for the occasionally dirty competition of the business world. For long-term success, though, make a point of learning to be more yielding and responsive to those who work with and for you. Involve them in your decisions and you'll win their loyalty forever.

Money

Your finances are the source of your self-esteem, so it's a given that you've got a full portfolio, from bank accounts to retirement plan. But your tendency to value money above all else puts you at risk for making foolish moves in search of big financial gains. You may be at the top of the pile one day, King Midas, but your avarice may lead you to a great fall. When you're making your lofty plans, a little dose of moderation can be key to your financial success.

Health and Fitness

Fitness is the ideal outlet for releasing the tension that perpetually builds up inside most Eights. Before it begins to wreak havoc on your body (you're prone to migraines, back problems, heart disease), you need to establish a daily routine that helps you get rid of stress. Any kind of competitive sport where you can work up a sweat should do the trick—squash, racquetball, basketball. Eights tend to have a macho attitude toward their bodies. You may find yourself pushing too hard, or when you're sick, thinking you can "sweat it out" through a good workout. Remind yourself to ease up instead. Let illness run its course peacefully. Your more-is-better attitude extends toward food as well. You may tend to overeat or overindulge, so you need to learn the benefits of delayed gratification and a nutritious diet. Take the time to seek out healthier foods—your body will thank you for it in the long run.

How to Recognize an Eight

Remember those old E. F. Hutton commercials? Well, when an Eight walks into a room, everyone listens. There's a hush, except for a few whispers of acknowledgment of your power, and all heads turn to look and stare. The style and cut of your clothing grabs attention; there's a great gravity to your appearance and and an unapologetic certainty in your gait.

Famous Eights

Warren Beatty, Matt Damon, Anthony Edwards, Richard Gere, Ben Stiller, Barbra Streisand, Tori Spelling

Nines

Walk into the home of a Nine and you'll probably see a poster of Mother Teresa on the wall. And another over the desk. Nines are humanitarians, driven by their sense of ethical obligation to give back to the world, and to leave it a slightly better place than when they found it. You feel deeply for people less fortunate than you, and are eager to help out in any way that you can. But your bottomless generosity leaves you vulnerable to being taken advantage of. Your boundless idealism is your greatest strength, but also your greatest weakness.

Strengths

High-minded, compassionate, selfless, and creative

Weaknesses

Manipulative, deceptive, conceited, and unstable

Overall Self-improvement Goals

To do good for others without neglecting your own emotional needs along the way

Romance

Nines are die-hard romantics who fall in and out of love with ease and frequency. Your eyes meet those of another across the room, and your heart has been won. Nines look for partners who are equally passionate and equally inspiring. But you have to be wary of getting lost in your passions, since you tend to jump into any relationship blindly. You can work toward being a better mate by becoming more temperate, flexible, and considerate of your partner.

Friendship

Nines are very social and make friends easily; people are attracted to your warm, engaging personality. You seek out friends who are just as noble minded and sensitive as you are. Because of your giving nature, you need to be careful not to let others take advantage of your willingness to part with the shirt on your back. To preserve your self-worth, be more realistic about your limitations and focus more on the realities of the here and now instead of the uncertainties of the future.

Work

As a Nine, you're ideally suited for any kind of workplace in which you can exercise your generosity of spirit and creative muscle. Perfect careers are those in the arts—writing, painting, music—as well as the clergy (organized or alternative religions), education, or charity work. The business world is not for you, since your fundraising skills could be easily abused or misdirected.

Money

Despite your deep disdain for money, you need to learn to think of its practical uses. You can't support good causes if you don't have anything to give in the first place. Remember, earning and saving money doesn't make you mercenary; we all need money for shelter, food, and clothing. Be especially wary, too, of high-flying ideas and schemes which you are especially vulnerable to because of your selflessness.

Health and Fitness

With all their energy devoted so completely to spiritual health, Nines can't be bothered with the mundane notion of physical fitness. So to stay in shape, try looking for good causes such as an AIDS bike ride or a walk for breast cancer, something that offers improved social conditions and spiritual insight while increasing your fitness. Nines can be completely caught up in the need to end world hunger, while at the same time completely ignoring their own needs—you tend to eat only when you're reminded to do so. Force yourself to become more aware of what you're eating, and make sure you're filling all your nutritional needs, so that you can stay strong enough to save the world.

How to Recognize a Nine

With your head always in the clouds, you look as though you could lift off at any moment. Nines are always cheery and upbeat, but also a bit ethereal.

Famous Nines

Patricia Arquette, Jim Carrey, Kirsten Dunst, Harrison Ford, Anthony Hopkins, Courtney Love, Renée Zellweger

Best and Worst Matches

One
Best: Six
Worst: Three

Two
Best: Four
Worst: Nine

Three
Best: Five
Worst: Eight

Four
Best: Six
Worst: One

Five
Best: Three
Worst: Seven

Six
Best: Eight
Worst: Two

Seven
Best: Six and Two
Worst: Five

Eight

Best: Four
Worst: Five

Nine

Best: Four
Worst: Three

8

All the Rest

*I*n calling this book *The Ultimate Personality Guide,* we set out to explore some of the most interesting and effective systems of typology. Indeed, in the seven previous chapters you've seen the many ways in which experts from a variety of disciplines—from modern psychology to ancient philosophy—are able to analyze our personalities. Inevitably, though, we had to leave out many good, equally compelling systems. There's simply no way we could include all of them and still make this a book you could carry around without landing you in traction. So, after we'd selected seven of the most popular systems for in-depth exploration in these pages, we decided to highlight some of the others here. Think of this chapter as an antipasto of personality systems. If any of these teasers tempt you, you can order the main-course version—we'll list some other books to help you explore the subject in greater depth.

Essential Elements

The idea of a typology based on "essential elements" relates back to Chinese astrology (Chapter Six). The Chinese calendar rotates not only on a twelve-year cycle of animals, as you learned, but also on a five-year cycle of elements: fire, water, metal, earth, and wood. As with your "animal," your element is determined by the date of your birth, and influences your personality by driving it with a specific, "element"-dependent kind of energy.

Fire

2/12/56–2/17/58; 1/21/66–1/29/68; 1/31/76–2/6/78

If you're born under the element of fire, passion is said to be your driving force. You're adventurous, joyful, innovative, and decisive; your boundless charisma has won you many friends and admirers. But your gift for drawing others to you works in both directions; the sheer force of your will can push people away as easily as it attracts them. You can be sharp-tongued when you're hurt or angry, and if you find no better outlet for your anger, your intensely passionate nature can direct it inward, causing you to indulge in self-destructive behaviors like overeating or alcohol abuse.

Water

2/5/62–2/12/64; 2/15/72–1/22/74; 1/25/82–2/1/84

You're a wise, calm person who's known for your vast knowledge and deep, philosophical ideas. Your flexible nature and gifts of persuasion allow you to ease in and out of tense situations, and others rely on you to soothe their frayed nerves. But in your efforts to keep the peace, you can be too conciliatory. You may tend to give in to others at the expense of your own needs.

Metal

1/28/60–2/4/62; 2/6/70–2/14/72; 2/16/80–1/24/82

As a person ruled by metal, you're ambitious and energetic, tirelessly working toward whatever goals you've set for yourself. Others enjoy your company because you're so dependable and clear-eyed. But your trademark persistence can also turn into stubbornness. You have a tendency to be somewhat inflexible, narrow-minded, even austere. You don't relax easily, and your colleagues probably call you a workaholic.

Earth

2/18/58–1/27/60; 1/30/68–2/5/70; 2/7/78–2/15/80

The expression "salt of the earth" suits people born in earth years perfectly. You're honest (to a fault), hardworking, and unfailingly responsible. You've got a good head on your shoulders, and a strong sense of balance and stability. But your powerful self-discipline tends to rob you of any imagination or adventure. You're too quick to give up a night on the town with friends in exchange for a few hours spent at home, diligently balancing your checkbook.

Wood

2/3/54–2/11/56; 2/13/64–1/20/66; 1/23/74–1/30/76;
2/2/84–2/8/86

Those born in wood years are typically dignified, elegant lovers of beauty and the arts. Your self-confidence comes not from egotism but from your generous spirit and love of life. Others respect you for your compassionate and understanding nature.

However, you have a tendency to take on more than even you can handle, and you may lash out in anger or frustration as a result. Your confidence means that you know what you want, and you may act with cunning or force in order to get your way.

Color

Quick: What's your favorite color? What color is most prominent in your wardrobe, your home, or your office? Some believe that the colors with which we choose to surround ourselves can offer valuable insight into our personality.

Color typology can be drawn from a number of roots, one of which is the ancient Sanskrit system of chakras. According to its practitioners, the body has seven energy systems, or chakras, each with its own life force and each identified by a color of its own. The seven chakras are red (earth chakra); orange (water chakra); yellow (power chakra); green (heart chakra); blue (sound chakra); indigo (third eye chakra); and violet (crown chakra). Each of us has all seven chakras; what differs among us is the relative strength of each and their balance to one another. That balance determines our personality—and our potential.

But that's not the only typology theory surrounding colors. Here's what some other psychologists have to say about the subject:

Red

Red is the color of power (remember Nancy Reagan's attention-grabbing scarlet suits?). If you love the color red, you're probably a person who is bursting with strength, vitality, and the courage of your convictions. You want things done your way, and you won't settle for anything less. You're someone who always has to be right, and you'll never admit it if you're not. You want others to respect you for your intelligence and depth of knowledge, and for that reason you often land in leadership jobs—like judge or politician—where you can get all the approval and adulation that you crave.

Orange

If your favorite color is orange, you probably have an independent streak a mile wide—you're a free spirit with enviable talents of creativity. You enjoy being spontaneous, and your life is one long relentless pursuit of happiness; you never know when you wake up in the morning what road you'll follow or where the day will take you. Your enthusiasm is contagious and has won you devoted friends and followers—despite your innate restlessness in the face of commitment and relationships.

Yellow

You're driven by your sense of adventure. To you, life is a party, and you don't want to miss a minute of it. And you want to make sure no one misses you, either. (How could they, when your sunny ensembles stand out in a crowd?) You need to be noticed, to be popular, and to have the approval of others, so that they can admire you as you regale them with your fun-filled tales. But deep down you know that life is more than just fun and games—you're also something of an intellectual who loves learning new things. And sometimes all that knowledge can make you a bit overanxious and fretful. There is such a thing as too much information.

Green

Green is the color of nature and the environment, and that's indeed a cause that's very important to you. But it's just one of many, because you're a giving, caring person with a huge, open heart. You're unfailingly benevolent and humanistic—truly a committed soul. You're a generous lover and friend, dispensing love and attention at every turn. Be careful, though, to guard yourself against those who might take advantage of your good nature and pervert it toward their own less charitable motives.

Blue

You're a sensitive person with high moral principles and infinite patience, especially for those you love. Motivated by altruism and integrity, you love to help others, and seek out their affection in return. You value intimacy above all else and would readily sacrifice everything you have—career and all—for the promise of true love. But you tend to be overly emotional, falling in and out of love time and again, having your heart broken by those who are less open and sincere than you.

Purple

Traditionally the color of choice for royalty, purple signals an artistic, creative spirit. If you love purple, then you're probably a person who's set big goals for yourself—you want to get as much as you can out of life, and your ample talents will help get you there. But your gifts also may bring you a less-than-humble sense of your self. You tend to be somewhat pompous and arrogant when it comes to your abilities. Some may complain that you're rather impatient and rude when you don't get your way.

White

If white is your favorite color, you're an optimistic, patient person who enjoys doing your own thing. Motivated by a need to keep the peace, you'll do anything to avoid confrontation. Some may call you passive, but you're not weak—you'll readily stand up for yourself if you feel the situation calls for it. You resent being scolded or criticized, and you don't like to be ordered or pushed around by others. You're far more responsive to suggestions rather than demands. What's most important to you is feeling good about yourself and the life that you're living.

Blood Types

How can your blood type possibly have anything relevant to say about your personality? Good question. Well, researchers have actually found certain correlations between health issues and a person's blood type. And as we saw with Ayurveda (Chapter Five), your health can indeed influence your personality in significant ways.

If you know your blood type (try checking your blood donor card, if you have one), refer to the list below to learn the characteristics associated with it.

Type A

You're meticulous in all that you do, often to a fault. You're a perfectionist, the type of person who plans everything, to the last detail, as far in advance as possible. Spontaneity is a dirty word as far as you're concerned; you'd rather sit home alone than do anything on impulse. You're also extremely sensitive and communal; you enjoy the company of others—just as long as it's on a set schedule.

Type B

You're far more creative than Type As; and you have a more flexible and empathetic nature that allows you to adapt easily to new situations. But you're also wildly unpredictable, making up your own rules as you go along, which can be challenging for your friends, partners, and colleagues. Your mood may swing from one moment to the next, and you lose interest in things seemingly overnight.

Type O

If you have type O blood, which is the most prevalent type, you're said to be a born leader and a go-getter, driven by your ambition to attain ever-growing levels of success and accomplishment. You're focused, self-reliant, and adventurous. What matters most to you are promotions, awards, even the notches on your bedpost. You're not content to simply be good at what you do—you have to be the best.

Type AB

Type AB is the rarest of all blood types, and as a result, you're something of an enigma. You're full of life and energy, which makes you very popular socially. But you're also intensely spiritual, which has earned you a reputation for being somewhat flaky. You rely more on impulse than on reason to guide you through life, from love and friendship to work and money.

Palmistry

According to the ancient system of palmistry, your future is literally in your hands—in the lines, the shapes, the forms of your palms. Your left hand reveals the characteristics you were born with; the right, the characteristics you've acquired as you've gone through life. The depth, length, and shape of the three most important lines—heart, head, and life—paint a complete portrait of your personality and hold predictions for your future. As you read through the descriptions below, compare the lines on your left, then your right hand to see where you've come from—and where you're heading.

Heart Line

Your heart line (which starts below your index finger and extends across the width of your palm, ending below your pinky finger) reflects not your romantic future but your approach to love. A straight line means you're passive in matters of the heart, waiting for love to come to you; a curved line means you aggressively seek out love. (Take a guess which type of line is more common with which gender. Hint: Men are historically hunters.)

Head Line

Your head line (which starts at the base of your index finger, below your heart line, and also runs across the width of your palm) shows how you think, not how intelligent you are. A short head line means you make quick decisions; a longer head line means you spend time to explore issues and think things through. A straight head line means you concentrate on what you know and what's been proven; a curved line means you're more creative and willing to experiment with new ideas.

Life Line

The life line (which starts at the base of your index finger along with your head line, but then runs down your palm) doesn't show how long you'll live, but how well. The deeper the line, the more energy and good health you now enjoy. If it runs close to your thumb, you're probably lagging in strength and energy. If it has a wide curve, you've got much more energy and vitality. If it's chained (an interlocking group of lines), you're likely to suffer from delicate health.

Handwriting

Your penmanship can also be a way of interpreting your character. The strokes, the slants, the shapes, even which hand you predominantly use to write with reveals a great deal about your personality: your aspirations, fantasies, yearnings, values, spirituality. In Europe, many companies use graphology (the art of handwriting analysis) to evaluate potential hires. (Seriously!) We may all have started out being taught the same way to write (remember the formal Palmer method?), but as our personalities evolved, so did our handwriting.

On a blank, unlined piece of paper, write a sentence or two about anything. (Need a suggestion? Try this: *and so, my fellow Americans, ask not what your country can do for you; ask what you can do for your country.*) Write in your normal, everyday style, as if you were taking notes for yourself. Then analyze your penmanship according to the principles given below.

Pen Pressure

Flip over the paper you just wrote on. Did your writing make an indentation through the other side of the sheet? Or can you barely tell that there's writing on the other side? If you write with strong pressure, you enjoy good health and vitality. Too much pressure is said to indicate aggressive behavior; too little, poor health.

Letter Shape

Those who write with rounded letters are often emotional, warmhearted people. Those who write with angular letters rely more on reason than on feelings; they're good organizers and managers.

Capital Letters

If you write them in the ornate style we learned in school, you're said to be reluctant to challenge authority. If you've abandoned that style in favor of simple block letters, you're said to be a free-thinker and a nonconformist.

Slant

If your letters slant to the right, you're an extrovert; if they slant to the left, you're more introverted and shy. If your sentences go uphill, you're an optimist; if they go downhill, you're more of a pessimist.

Spacing

The amount of space between your words reflects your level of connection to other people. A lot of space may mean that you're afraid of intimacy; crowding your words together can mean that you're too needy and clingy.

Afterword

We hope you enjoyed this book and learned at least something new you hadn't known about yourself (or your friends!) before.

If you'd like to find out more about any of the subjects we've touched on here, we recommend the following books, which offer more in-depth analysis.

For Further Reading

Western Astrology

Astrology for Yourself: How to Understand and Interpret Your Own Birth Chart. Berkeley, CA: Wingbow Press, 1987
by Douglas Bloch

The Astrology Kit: Everything You Need to Cast Horoscopes for Yourself, Your Family and Friends. New York: St. Martin's Press, 1988
by Grant Lewi, Liz Greene

Alan Oken's Complete Astrology. Toronto: New York: Bantam Doubleday Dell, 1989 Pub. (Trade pap)
by Alan Oken

Astrology for the Soul. New York: Bantam Books, 1997
by Jan Spiller

Birth Order

The Birth Order Challenge: Expanding Your Horizons. Upper Des Moines, 1991
by Clifford E. Isaacson

Everything You Need to Know about Birth Order. New York: Rosen Publishing Group, 2000
by Katherine Krohn

The New Birth Order Book: Why You Are the Way You Are. Grand Rapids, MI: Fleming H. Revell Co., 1998
by Kevin Leman

Myers-Briggs–Inspired Typology

Dancing the Wheel of Psychological Types. Wilmette, IL: Chivon Pubns., 1991
by Mary E. Loomis

Personality Types: Jung's Model of Typology. Toronto, Canada: Inner City Books, 1987
by Daryl Sharp

Jung's Typology in Perspective. Wilmette, IL: Chivon Pubns., 1995
by Angelo Spoto

Personality Type: An Owner's Manual. Boston: Shambhala Pubns., 1998
by Lenore Thomson

The Enneagram

The Enneagram Made Easy: Discover the Nine Types of People. Harper San Francisco, 1994
by Renée Baron, Elizabeth Wagele

The Spiritual Dimension of the Enneagram: Nine Faces of the Soul. New York: JP Tarcher, 2000
by Sandra Maitri

The Wisdom of the Enneagram: The Complete Guide to Psychological and Spiritual Growth for the Nine Personality Types. New York: Bantam Doubleday Dell Pub. (Trd Pap), 1999
by Don Richard Riso, Russ Hudson

Ayurveda

Ayurveda: The Science of Self-Healing. Santa Fe, NM: Lotus Press, 1984
by Vasant D. Lad

The Ayurveda Encyclopedia: Natural Secrets to Healing, Prevention, and Longevity. Bayville, New York: Ayurveda Holistic Center Press, 1998
by Swami Sada Shiva Tirtha

Chinese Astrology

The Handbook of Chinese Horoscopes. San Francisco: HarperCollins (paper), 1995
by Theodora Lau

Chinese Astrology: Plain and Simple. Boston: Charles E. Tuffle Co., 1998
by Suzanne White

The Animals of the Chinese Zodiac. Brooklyn, NY: Interlink Publishing Group, 1999
by Susan Whitfield

Numerology

Numerology: Key to Your Inner Self. Garden City Park, NY: Avery Pub., 1994
by Hans Decoz, Tom Monte

The Complete Illustrated Guide to Numerology. Boston: Element, 1999
by Sonia Ducie

Numerology: The Complete Guide. San Bernardino, CA: Borgo Press, 1982
by Matthew O. Goodwin

Color

What Color Is Your Aura: Personality Spectrums for Understanding and Growth. New York: Pocket Books, 1989
by Barbara Bowers

The Color Code: A New Way to See Yourself, Your Relationships, and Life. New York: Fireside, 1999
by Taylor Hartman, Ph.D., and Jean Hartman

What Color Is Your Personality? Red, Orange, Yellow, Green . . . Carlsbad, California: Hay House, 1999
by Carol Ritberger

Chakras

Wheel of Life
by Anodea Judith

Chakras, Energy Centers of Transformation
by Harish Johari

Blood Types

What's Your Type? How Blood Types Are the Keys to Unlocking Your Personality. New York: Plume, 1997
by Peter Constantine

Palmistry

Your Fate Is in Your Hands: Using the Principles of Palmistry to Change Your Life. New York: Pocket Books, 2000
by Donna McCue, Stacey Donovan

Art of Hand Reading. New York: DK Publishing, 1996
by Lori Reid

The Complete Book of Palmistry. New York: Bantam Books, 1983
by Joyce Wilson

Handwriting

The Complete Idiot's Guide to Handwriting Analysis. New York: Macmillan Distribution, 1999
by Sheila R. Lowe, June Canoles

Your Handwriting Can Change Your Life! New York: Fireside, 2000
by Vimala Rodgers

Better Handwriting. Lincolnwood, IL: Teach Yourself, 1994
by Rosemary Sassoon

About the Authors

Jennifer Freed, M.A., M.F.T., is a licensed marriage, family, and child therapist with twenty years of experience practicing psychotherapy. Founder of Astrological Counseling Seminars (www.jenniferfreed.com), an institute for astrological psychology, she is a professional astrologer who has been teaching the subject for eight years. She lives in Santa Barbara, CA.

Debra Birnbaum, former senior editor at *George* and deputy editor at *Redbook*, has written for numerous national publications, including *More, New Woman,* and *Men's Health.* She lives in New York City.